D1829186

I'm afraid this is a true story.

"I can't do anything for you except listen your story. That's all..." - Jun

Halfway gone – Life and Love after Stroke

ISBN 978-1-4709-4589-3

Part 1

Chapter 1

August 26th 2007 - 11 days to the crippling

Nakatsu, Osaka, Japan

Me and Jun are joshing. I'm sat on the stairs, three or four steps up. Jun's at the bottom, stood up in a fleecy orange dressing gown I'd bought for her. There's a sound of water running in the background and the fresh, lemon-y smell of a bath tablet dissolving in the water. The bathroom is tiny but it's a completely waterproof room, a place to take a shower and next to it a cramped, half-size bath. In the West it would be a "wet room" but that would be far too grand a name for what was just a typical bathroom here. Still I loved it and I loved that you had to get naked here in the stairwell before you went in. Engage Jun in some amusing banter at the right time and you would be rewarded with a glimpse of naked flesh as she went in. I'd been with Jun for years so the sight of her naked was hardly new to me but, hey, I still fancied my wife. Nothing wrong with that.

So we were joshing with each other. We had developed a game around birthday/Christmas/anniversary/Valentine's/White Day presents. The gift receiver could ask questions about the nature of the gift in a yes/no style and the gift giver had to reply. Had to reply but didn't have to reply truthfully. The art was to tantalise with your answers without giving too much away. The receiver would have a desired object in their head (new camera, piece of jewellery, leather wallet) and, as such, would tend to ask questions leading down a path towards that. The giver could dissemble, taunt and tease as much as they wanted and watch the recipient wriggle in anticipation. The rules, as much as either of us adhered to them, didn't really stop bare-faced lying and evil attempts at misdirection. At the back of both our minds was the security that neither of us had ever really messed up with a gift so we could mess about without too much fear of disaster. We hadn't yet been together long enough to have run out of things to give each other that were genuinely desired.

My best usage of the game so far had been when I was taking Jun on a surprise weekend away during one of our trips to England. She'd managed to wheedle out of me that the first letter of our holiday destination began with a "B". She assumed this meant we were going to a country that began with a "B" – Belgium? Belarus? Bulgaria? Bosnia?

All were wrong leaving her totally perplexed. There weren't anymore "B"s in Europe, were there? Surely you can't get to Brazil on easyJet? How I chuckled safe in the knowledge that we were going to Barcelona. Hoho! And I wasn't even lying! Jun was thinking countries and I, fresh from tortuous on-line navigations to book the flights, was thinking purely in cities. Much to my satisfaction the secret remained unrevealed until Jun opened a Barcelona guidebook on Christmas morning. We had an ace trip – Gaudi, pinxtos and the Nou Camp. I'd meant to propose during the trip but bottled it at the last minute.

But this time I was the one being tormented. It was my birthday in a few weeks and I was trying to deduce what my present was. We'd established it came from Paul Smith and Jun was trying to convince me that it was about A3 size and made of metal and leather. I was pretty dubious but worried that if I expressed too much incredulity – "Who could possibly want something like that" – only to actually receive something that fitted those seemingly ridiculous descriptions I might look stupid and ungrateful and end up making Jun feel silly. Anyway I had a hunch she was lying. She had bought me a Paul Smith watch. I'd inflicted enough bored minutes in front of display cases for her to have got the message. To be any more obvious I would have to have written a message in the cabinet glass that was being steamed up by my yearning breath. I could have done it in English but I had no idea of the Japanese character for "watch". It seems silly now when I think about all that the watch means to me, but, at the time, ¥30,000 seemed a huge amount of money to spend.

Chapter 2

September 16th 2007 – 10 days since the crippling

Kaisei Hospital, Shin-Osaka, Osaka, Japan

It's my birthday. Cut-out cardboard letters, multi-coloured and shiny, spell "Happy Birthday". They are hung between two hospital stands. The kind that drips would usually be suspended from. I look at the drip going into my arm and follow the tube up and further up until I see my own drip pack, hung from another stand. That makes three around me – one pumping something translucent and sticky looking into my arm and two bearing birthday greetings. The nurses have done this especially for me. It's not normal procedure and they are pleased at their ingenuity.

My parents are at the end of the bed. They smile uncertainly and had me a gift. I tear at the wrapping paper ineffectually with one hand – no! I don't need any help. That's what it's supposed to sound like anyway. God knows what the actual noises resemble. It's a whiskey glass, threateningly heavy in my hand. It's a nice present – I've just got into drinking single malt whiskey but I have no idea when I'll get to use it or even when I'll be able to have another drink.

Jun steps forward and hands me a small box. I wish my parents weren't here to watch me open it. I claw it open and it is the watch I'd hoped for. Stainless steel and discrete, it has four small discs cut out of the face, two by "3 o'clock" and two by "9 o'clock". Most of the face is black but underneath it is another disc made up of greens, blues, purples and reds. This disc rotates in time with the second hand and every 15 seconds a new colour appears visible beneath the black. Two shades of green by "3 o'clock" and two shades of red by "9 o'clock" then, after the sweep of the second hand moves a quarter around its perimeter, purples and blues. Four different colours a minute – always changing yet never changing. I spend vast amounts of time over the next few weeks watching the colours change. That and the vacuous shapes on the TV the only movement I'll see for hours. Me and Jun exchange giggles about her pitiful attempts at misdirection and I unsuccessfully attempt to explain the game to my parents.

The watch is taken off its holder. Jun hands it to me. My left arm and hand is utterly immobile but I slip the watch over my wrist with my right hand. It looks good close to my wedding ring. I thank Jun in Japanese and tell her I love her, glad my parents don't understand and I can gush a little. She gives me a hug and leaves with my parents.

I understand conceptually that Jun can't stay with me every minute of every day but now she's gone I'm lonely and scared. I look at the watch on my left wrist and feel a tiny sense of solace.

I send a message from my brain to lift and twist my wrist so the watch face is visible. Nothing happens. My fingers, thumb, wrist, elbow and shoulder haven't moved for ten days.

It's my birthday. I have no history of ill health. I don't have high blood pressure. I gave up smoking years ago. I like a drink but not to excess. I'm not overweight. I do a pretty active job, cycle whenever I can and play sport most weekends. Ten days ago I had a massive stroke. I've just turned 36.

I reach down and use my right hand to grasp my left. Use one arm to lift and twist the totally unresponsive other one to bring the watch into view. I think I had wanted to know the time but tears cover my eyes and blur my vision. I can't see the hands or the changing colours.

Chapter 3

September 6th 2007 – the day of the crippling

Nakatsu, Osaka, Japan

"Down I go"

The day my life changed forever began just like any other. Get up, wash my hair, brush my teeth, feed the cat, set the coffee going, get dressed, have a stroke. My life snapped in a split second. There was no gradual descent into anything. One moment I'm stood at the sink doing last night's washing up and then a moment later I'm lying on the floor losing half my body. No warning, no gradually increasing feeling of there being something wrong. I had a slight headache but that was a fairly common occurrence first thing in the morning – too little sleep or that extra whiskey the night before.

I'm stood at the sink and I'm fine and then a micro-moment later my legs just collapse from underneath me. I don't collapse straight downwards but backwards and to my left. No, that's not it. "Collapse" isn't the right word. It implies a kind of gradual crumbling that didn't happen. I just went down, a straight-legged timber felling. One moment I was a vertical concept, now I'm a horizontal shape on the floor. It's happened in a heartbeat but it shouldn't be happening. I'm there where I should be and then, a second later, I'm on the floor and everything is wrong. One moment everything is alright and then, the next moment, nothing is ever going to be right ever again. The molecules above me in the shape I should be occupying seem to vibrate a silent accusation. I'm lying arms at angles and legs outstretched. Ready for the chalk outline. Usually if you trip or fall there is an obvious causal element involved. "I should have watched out for that curb" or "I should have been careful of those steps". There's something that it can be attributed to. There was nothing like this. I was standing up and then I was lying on the floor.

And all I can think of is The Simpsons. In one early episode Hans Moleman, the recurring shrivelled, myopic oldster, pulls out a huge knife in a parody of that "Call that a knife? *This* is a knife!" bit of Crocodile Dundee. The knife is so massive and Moleman is so feeble that the blade overbalances him and he topples over. This sprung into my mind as I went down. Hans doesn't struggle in any way. He just accepts his fate and the unavoidable fall. Rather than struggle against something that's as unavoidable as it is unexpected he just passes comment on it instead – "Down I go". That was all I could think of at the moment. There was no fight in me and no possibility of sustaining verticality. Unfortunately there was no one nearby to hear my witty allusion but I thought it and then down I went.

I wasn't scared. I wasn't even that surprised. What had happened seemed so bizarre that I didn't really know what to think. People faint or pass out. I'd seen that kind of thing in films but never in real life and, anyway, I was still conscious. People who passed out in films were unconscious and needed some space or slapping to bring them round. I found myself on the floor but wide awake. I may even have thought "Wow! This is serious enough that I can take the day off and not feel guilty". I'm on the floor. What should I do now? I know I should maybe think about getting up again but the rust-coloured lino is smooth and cool on my cheek. My head rests on its side on the floor and the world looks familiarly unfamiliar at 90°. I quite like it down here but I know I ought to move. For a start, nausea is rising unstoppably along my throat. Not trusting my legs I try to crawl on all fours across the kitchen floor into the toilet. That works and I prop myself up on the bowl. The sick comes straight away. There is no food in there. I don't know what is going on but I'm fairly sure that this isn't a stomach bug. The vomit is a dull white colour like watery milk. When I have too much time to think in later endless hospital nights I imagine that this was liquidised brain. I vomit copiously but I don't feel any better. I'm not really in any pain but I can tell something is wrong. Why can't I stand up?

I crawl back into the kitchen and manage to lever myself up on the sink. It always strikes me as weird that in that moment when I was unknowingly as near to death as I have ever been that bits of my body still worked. I crawled quite happily that morning but I can't crawl now. I stood up on my own by the sink – that kind of thing took me months of physio to achieve after today. It's strange that this process that seemed to ruin me instantaneously actually took some minutes to wreak its havoc. I turned on the tap and drank a glass of water. I normally preferred some Britta water out of the fridge but it looked an ocean away at this moment. The water is refreshing but I need to find a way to get into the downstairs living room and lie down. I'm don't trust my body to support my weight so I make a graceless tumble to the floor and crawl into the other room.

I position myself under the air conditioner, pull my work bag towards me by the strap and root through the vast array of pockets and compartments until I find my work mobile. I call the coordinator in

Tokyo and explain that I won't be in today but I should be in tomorrow. I can still speak but the mental effort it suddenly seems to require makes me feel as though my brain is going to explode. Japanese staff would rarely take a day off through illness and the "unreliable" Westerners taking sick days at the slightest sign of a sniffle are a big problem for my company. I don't think the nice woman in a Tokyo office quite believes that I'm sick. I have an almost endless capacity to feel guilty about stuff. Why did I call work in the middle of all this? I like to put it down to my unrelenting sense of responsibility towards my co-workers even as I departed their company. Either that or being so utterly in thrall to The Man that I felt I couldn't possibly let him down. I think part of my thinking was because I had no way of calibrating this morning. I could guess that this was worse than a cold but I really had no experience with which I could compare this. I'd never had a stroke before.

My only thought now was to call Jun. She was good. She helped me when I had a problem. That was what I did. If I had a problem I talked to Jun. She couldn't always help but if she could she would. I found my personal mobile in my dressing gown pocket and called Jun. She was at her parents' shop at this time of the morning. She answered. Speaking was harder now. I felt as though I was having to physically push the word-forming messages from my brain to my tongue.

"Help me. Help me. Help me." I croaked. I couldn't manage Japanese.

Jun, to her eternal credit, didn't say -

"Take the day off work, relax and I'll see you tonight."

She didn't say –

“I’ve got to go to work but call me in an hour if you still feel bad.”

She said –

“I’m coming straight home. I won’t be too long.”

Thinking about things later I should perhaps have called an ambulance first. I didn’t know I was having a stroke but speed of treatment makes a big difference in how bad strokes are. I didn’t think at the time. I just wanted Jun with me. She was my conduit and guide into so many parts of life and I wanted her here. I didn’t know at the time that I was entering another life completely. Jun texted me a few minutes later. She was on the train and would be back in an hour or so. Just hang tight.

I was scared now. Something was clearly very wrong. I was lying head on the sofa body on the floor. I was extremely hot even directly under the blast of the air-conditioner and nauseous. Vomiting hadn’t helped. There were lumps of sick on my dressing gown. None of my body felt like it worked. Limbs were too heavy and there seemed to be a weight on my chest pressing me down. It occurred to me that I didn’t know what dying felt like and this could be it. I didn’t want to die. It was my birthday soon and I thought Jun had got me a Paul Smith watch. I wasn’t in any pain but everything felt wrong. I could breath but I felt as though I had to think about it. Jun wouldn’t be home for an hour or so I tried to settle down. I knew you weren’t supposed to go to sleep in situations like this but I would have been happy to slip away if my body had let me. My eyes were as busy as the rest of my body was suddenly useless. They Eagle Eyed around the room as the rest of me lay there unable to move. At one point Sai poked his head around the door but just as quickly turned and fled. His sensitive nose must have been picked up the scent of a massive imbalance in the natural order of things. The smell of "all wrong" in his nostrils, rotten and reeking, drove him away.

Time passed. I existed in between two worlds. I could hear people outside the window on the way to work. Morning greetings were exchanged. Bicycle bells tinkled. I wasn't of that world anymore. Lying immobile on the floor I felt like I was nothing but pure consciousness. I felt no serenity, no peace. I was scared. I just wanted things back the way they were. I wanted to catch the train to Hyotanyama and go and teach my lessons.

Jun arrived back and saved my life. I was starting to drift until the key in the lock snapped me back. This is something that stays with me – how close was I to slipping away completely? What if I had gone, just gone? When I initially fell over I was in the relative expanse of our kitchen so probably the worse place I could have found myself was face down in the litter tray but if everything had happened a minute earlier I would have been in the toilet and my head could have easily smashed into the toilet bowl or the edge of the sink and left me badly injured on top of everything. This was unimaginably bad but it could have been even worse. Jun took one look at me and called an ambulance. Then she got me a glass of water and gave me a hug. I was sick again a few moments later. The ambulance took perhaps 15 minutes to arrive and all the time her reassuring words and presence helped me stay calm.

By the time the ambulance arrived I was drifting in and out of consciousness pretty badly. I had blurry tableaux of things happening to me, brief sense memories. There were two ambulance men in green overalls. They may well have hard hats on. They did medical stuff to me and then lugged me to the ambulance. I remember clearly that the stretcher they carried me out on wasn't rigid. They somehow levered me into this floppy, shapeless thing and carted me outside. It felt all wrong, somewhere between a hammock and a body bag. The hospital wasn't too far away but lying on my back and feeling every turn made the journey pretty horrific. We arrived but I was barely aware of what was happening. Jun told a doctor that I was a gaijin[1] but I could understand Japanese. I couldn't really understand anything at that point. Jun was ushered away and I was carried into a sparkling treatment room. Nausea was rising again. It was awash with mysterious and impressive looking equipment but nowhere that looked like somewhere to be sick. It didn't really matter. Very soon I wouldn't have any choice about where it went. The expression on my face made it pretty clear what I was going to do imminently. The doctor and the nurses scanned the room frantically for a suitable receptacle. They settled on a reformed cardboard kidney bowl. It looked woefully small and it turned out that it was.

The next week was a fitful fever dream. Jun held my hand sometimes. Sometimes I was alone. Sometimes nurses clustered around me. Sometimes my parents kept vigil at the end of the bed and sometimes it was Jun's. Sometimes I didn't care. Sometimes I was scared. Sometimes I kicked and howled. Sometimes I accepted everything with a quiet resignation. Machines I couldn't bring into focus bleeped and whirred around me. Drips emptied into my veins. I tried to talk to Jun but my lips wouldn't form words. A few moments of lucidity were scattered into those dark days. I didn't think I would ever leave that

---

[1]外人- non-Japanese, a foreigner.

dimly-lit room. I had a sense of the size of the room and my solitude within it, even though I couldn't bring anything into focus I could make out shapes and outlines well enough to see that I was the only patient in a large room. I could sense the empty space that surrounded me. I'd been in hospital here before and I'd been crammed into a bay in a room sharing a sink and a window with three other patients. No windows here. The quantity of equipment spread about the room that seemed exclusively for my use was foreboding. So much of that week in the I.C.U. is a blur but I remember as clear as today the moment when I became sensate enough to realise what had happened to me. Lying in the bed I tested my limbs out of nothing more than a desire to stretch my limbs. My right leg was fine but the left leg doesn't move at all. Suddenly I was concentrating there. Sending a ball of consciousness from my head down my torso. The balls sparkled and whirred as they made their way down my body. Once at their destination I willed them into place scaffolding muscles and pulling sinews tight. Now, with my auxiliary forces in place everything would be OK. I tried to lift my leg. Nothing happened. Panic rising I concentrated hard and willed the leg to rise. Nothing. Over the course of the next few minutes I got out of breath trying differing strategies to get things to move. I could send the message down from brain perfectly. I could sense neural pathways tingling. Messages departed from my head with bullet train efficiency but then stalled somewhere around my crotch and never reached the destination. Feeling was no problem. Exploratory pinches lead to frantic slaps. I could feel every one. Perhaps violence could terrify it into doing what a leg should do? The skin wrapper was fine but the inside was hollow. Next I strained everything and tried to get the thing to move. Teeth gritted, a pearl of sweat appearing on my brow, I dared my body to defy me. It stared me down unblinkingly and lay motionless. Next, remembering how normally my body required no conscious thought to move, I though I could maybe my fool myself into compliance. If you have an itchy nose you just scratch it rather than thinking about clenching and loosening the particular muscles needed to get a finger up to your nose. Moving my still extant right leg just happened. I was kicking out in frustration or banging down on the mattress with each thwarted exertion. That required no thought perhaps so I was just overthinking things? I turned my head to one side and very deliberately thought about different things – Shunsuke's free kicks against Man U in the Champion's League this season, the mushrooms in garlic oil from that tapas place we liked, those Chimays waiting for me in the fridge when I got home. Then, all of a sudden, I'd ever so surreptitiously try to move my leg. The working part of my body aimed to trick my non-working part into behaving correctly. "Oh yeah! I'm looking forward to those beers when I get back home. I think I'll just cross my legs in recreation of how I'll relax on the sofa...there we go." Despite not being able to manage basic movements anymore my body was not *that* easily fooled. Nothing moved and my leg lay obstinately inert.

Over the next ten minutes I strained and cursed. My arm was the same – nothing. I had no context for anything that was happening to me. I was in a hospital, serious looking machines beeped ominously around me. I seemed to have lost the ability to speak coherently. My left leg and arm wouldn't move. I was more scared than I'd ever been before. Not "what am I going to do with my life now?" scared but "What is happening to me? Am I going to die?" scared. I was trapped in this strange body. I could see that it was mine but it didn't feel like me. My left side couldn't be me anymore. My left side worked.

Time was fairly meaningless here but I guessed it was night. The room was dimmed and there were no nurses visible. I was alone. I'd seen people I knew and loved since I'd collapsed but I had no idea where they were now or if they'd ever come again. This felt like the world I'd lived in for 35 years but it could be anywhere. What if my blasé atheism was wrong and I was somewhere else, some other plane? This didn't feel like a dream. It felt real. I was awake. Even if I couldn't see too well my other senses were pinpoint. There was a layer of realism far beyond any dream I had had before. The hospital blankets felt heavy on my chest, I could smell the bleach that must have been used recently to scrub the floor and I could hear the regular squeals of the machines I was hooked up to. As much as I wanted a get out clause – "Jun! This dream I had last night was so scary! You won't believe it!" – there was none to be found. This was me now.

I had become dimly aware of what I had become. Tears and cornered snarls were coming out now. My breath was coming in short, hot pants as I became more hysterical. My body writhed, stiffened and flopped in time to my howls. Breath heaved in and out faster and more frantic with each suck. I was hyperventilating, choking on my tears. I have never been less self-conscious before or after. This was pure terror. I was trapped in myself.

As much as my wailing was intended for no one but myself it had attracted the attention of a nurse. She came into my room and asked me what was wrong. I don't think I managed to reply in anything approaching words just clench-teethed groans and sweaty frustration. The nurse must have spent a few minutes by my bedside trying to get me to calm down but what can you really say? I had lost the use of half my body but the remaining fleshy mass had stayed behind to taunt me.

I guess nurses aren't allowed to lie like anyone else in situations like this. "Everything's going to be alright." When, exactly? What does "everything" encompass, precisely?

What she could do was medicate me –

"Maybe Padmore-san would like something to help him sleep?"

Not really. This was my coming out party. "Matthew – meet Matthew" "Horrified to meet you". This sudden influx of information was mortifying and overwhelming. Still I took the offered pills. I was in hospital – you did what nurses suggested. A few minutes later my head started to sag and my neck began to unfurl. I was still horribly aware of what I had become but it seemed to be at a remove from me, at a tangent. My eyelids started to flutter. I didn't want to sleep. I had only just begun to understand what was happening and I needed time to process, to reboot. In a few minutes I had no choice.

Chapter 4

September 26th 2007 - 3 weeks since the crippling

Kaisei Hospital, Shin-Osaka, Osaka, Japan

The first few weeks in hospital were little more than a daze. I slept a lot. Jun came to visit often. The hospital was near our house so it was easy for her to get there. My parents spent a lot of time visiting. It was nice to see them but I got tired quickly. I knew where I was and I could tell which parts of my body did and didn't work but I didn't really understand what was happening to me. What was going on? Why was all this stuff happening? I didn't trust my speaking but every week I dutifully texted work and told them that I probably wouldn't be in that week. Meal times meant a lumbered swing from bed to wheelchair. Always supervised, of course, although what a petite Japanese female nurse would be able to do if I toppled I never quite understood. At least they would be on the spot to do first aid. Unless I toppled on top of them. Shower time was as embarrassing as it was refreshing. Being undressed, transferring naked from a normal wheelchair onto a shower chair, being washed and then redressed. I had lost a lot of weight over the last few weeks but my fledgling belly still bulged. Once, at the second hospital I was at, a nurse took in my naked carcass and said that I was obviously "one of those people who only look thin when they're dressed." Cheers for that. Luckily the lady who did the job here was old and crone-like. An unwanted stiffy would have been extremely embarrassing – another part of my body that I couldn't control. Western men are supposed to be well-endowed and I'm sure mine was the first white penis that most of the nurses had seen. I hope I didn't let anybody down.

As amusing as the motorised "bed goes up, bed goes down" thing was it lost its novelty after a few days and I was pretty glad when they said I could start some rehab. I had no idea what to expect when they tipped me into the wheelchair and rolled me to the lifts. We went down two floors and then they manoeuvred me round a corridor corner and through some double doors. The rehab room was fairly breathtaking, by far the biggest room I had been in for weeks. In reality it probably wasn't as expansive as it seemed in to my already institutionalised mind but it was pretty impressive. A squeaky parquet floor stretched in front of me. Scattered around the room were treatment tables maybe 6 foot square and 18 inches off the ground. Me and my therapist, Nishimura-sensei, would find a vacant spot, I would lunge from chair to table and once there her fingers would attempt to work their magic, flexing and stretching muscles and limbs. In one corner there was a mock up of a house and in another corner a set of stairs that led nowhere. There were various pulleyed and springed contraptions on the walls around the room. I couldn't work out what they were designed for at all – mysterious large metal shapes loomed around me. They were pristine, shiny and scratch-free, as though daring you to be messed up enough to need to use them. I expected that I would be the first.

In the beginning rehab was great. I didn't have to do anything, just lie there and be passive. The Nishimura-sensei was female, young and attractive, excited to be treating a gaijin. Nothing was expected of me. I was just going to be rubbed back to health. This was just a more extreme form of massage.

Then everything changed. They wanted me to do *things.* Everything they asked me to do was impossible. I couldn't do *anything*. Suddenly I was expected to roll over, stretch things out and even stand up. I hadn't stood up for three weeks. Even the concept of being upright was bizarre. The idea that this body could go from the horizontal to vertical, from left-to-right to up-and-down almost seemed an affront. I eventually managed it, swaying straight-legged and hoping the therapists wouldn't let go. Other exercise attempts were not so successful. Every day's session ended with the same exercise. I was made to sit on the edge of the therapy table, legs a couple of feet apart. This was ok but then they wanted me to put my head as near to the floor as I could between my legs. As my back bent down more and more blood rushed into my head. My view was of nothing but the cloth of my t-shirt and my consciousness prepared to tumble forward. I'd lost my sense of internal equilibrium and knew that I wouldn't be able to right myself if I lost balance. I feigned an attempt at playing along but I was so scared that I didn't push myself in the slightest. I had no gauge as to how I was getting on except that I wasn't better yet. The man who was presumably the head therapist was often sent to work with me. The other therapists would cluster around reverently, keen to see him work his magic. I could tell that this was meant to be something special. He'd try to get me to make various poses - chin in palms of hands, head at a jaunty angle or a Nazi salute with my left arm. I couldn't ever do any of these and he would leave us after a few minutes with a look on his face that implied that I hadn't tried hard enough and was an affront to his status. Could I not see that my unwillingness to regain a full range of movement was making him look bad in front of his underlings?

The other potential problem with the early days of my rehab sessions was that I was still having a drip of something in my arm twice-a-day. I wasn't really sure what was going in but it seemed important. Once the nurse had found a vein the bag would drip its opaque gloop into my arm. Once the needle was in it didn't really hurt but it took a long time – an hour or more of no sudden movements. Only having the one arm that worked and then being forced to be careful with it was a bind. Inevitably they would come and get me for rehab just as the drip started. We'd try to get me, the drip and the drip stand downstairs. The drip stand was on wheels as was I so that was no problem but keeping the tube connected to me was. It was like a party game or a stainless steel puzzle out of a Christmas cracker. Trying to manoeuvre me out of bed without tangling or stretching the cord. It was a conundrum of twisting and turning, of tubes passed over my head or under my legs. Once we got the whole affair downstairs we'd try to do some meaningful work around the tube. That pretty much meant something that involved me motionless. I remember once that we were working through our stuff when I noticed a circular red stain on the pale green vinyl of my table. The room and all its equipment was new enough to be spotless but here, catching my eye, was a spot. The mark lay there tempting me to touch. I dipped it in and it was strangely wet, staining my finger. It looked like...but it couldn't be, surely? The next mark was on the right thigh of my pyjama bottoms. Bigger this time it had mingled with the cloth and was now a darker purple. Resigned now I looked over to my arm. The needle was still in held down by surgical tape but crimson blood was pooling all round the insertion and occasionally drip-dropping onto the floor. There actually wasn't too much blood but I was horrified, Carrie befouling the gym. Nishimura-sensei frantically mopped me up and called someone to disinfect the floor. She frantically wheeled me back to the ward and got someone to reinsert the drip. Apparently my veins are difficult to find.

Chapter 6

September 29th 2007 - 2 weeks and 2 days since the crippling

Kaisei Hospital, Shin-Osaka, Osaka, Japan

It's Saturday afternoon. I'm flat on my back on the hospital bed. I'm wearing Japanese hospital clothes, baggy trousers and a short jacket thing that ties up like a dressing gown. The nurses are keen for me to get into some clothes from home. It will "cheer me up" and provide a psychological boost apparently. I'm not so sure. The strange hotchpotch of home wear, emergency buys and panic parcels from M&S I eventually end up wearing for the next 6 months don't make me feel much better. It's not as though I can just slip into my new jeans. Soon enough I will be retaught how to dress myself but at the moment I can't do it alone. I don't really want to wear home clothes here anyway. I don't see have any desire to attempt to normalise this situation. Anyway the hospital's clothes are pleasingly Japanese. I can almost pretend that I'm just spending time at an onsen[2].

Jun has spent the morning in the food hall at the Daimaru department store and now she is sharing some of the bounty with me. It's the Hokkaido fair over there so there are lots of goodies that are normally only available either from Hokkaido gift shops or after a hefty delivery

---

[2] 温泉- Hot Spring Resort

charge. First up are some “Shiroi Koibito”, inch square sponge sandwiches covering a lighter than air white chocolate filling. We bought them as gifts for ourselves and others when we went up there for a national holiday enhanced weekend but to see them readily available on the streets of downtown Osaka is a rarity. The name “Shiroi Koibito”[3] translates to “white sweetheart” or something similar presumably in reference to the white chocolate used but I always liked to think it referred to me. I was the “white sweetheart” in question and the biscuits were named after me – I’m “white” and Jun’s “sweetheart”, right? Whatever the origin of the name they are very morish and I was hoping the rest of the pack would end up in my fridge when Jun left.

Conversation topics were hard to find. I was either sleeping, waiting for a drip to finish dispensing unknown but presumably essential liquids into my arm or being pushed down to frustrating physio sessions. Jun was working her job, helping out at her parents’ dry cleaners before her real job, running the house and then coming to see me in the evenings. I was torn between needing her to spend as much time as possible with me (if I had my way I would have installed a double bed on the ward so she could sleep over) and recognising she must be falling over tired. The serious things that we had to say were far too big for words to encompass and everyday chit-chat was difficult when my recent day-to day experiences were rapidly becoming horrifically limited.

As such we soon fell to, what seemed to me, a portentous silence watching TV and holding hands. Weekend afternoon terrestrial TV in

---

[3] 白い恋人

Japan seemed extremely boring to me. Endless travelogues, cookery programs and a live broadcast of some guys racing up a mountain. As in many countries, the adverts were more entertaining. Short enough for Jun to explain and often with so little meaning that limited language proficiency was not a huge hindrance. Silly animations, daft costumes and slumming Hollywood types required little translation.

And then there was the music. Helpfully identified by a little caption on the bottom of the screen, it had turned me onto things that would become some of my favourites - "Strawberry Chips" by Halcali, "Time of the season" which led me to the many joys of "Odessey and Oracle".

This time it was a car advert for some kind of executive sedan. It swooped smoothly through the city shielding a tense salaryman from the horrors outside. The song he choose to vehicularly unwind to? "Whatever" by Oasis.

Now this is a song that I've always liked. Smack bang during Oasis's imperial phase, between the first two albums, but a non-album single that promoted nothing but itself and fell between the cracks as much as a single by a huge band can. Like most right thinking people I had lost interest with Oasis fairly quickly but there are gems hidden away in the dark corners of their catalogue. "Round Are Way", anyone?

My daily speech therapy seemed to be going well. As well as expected considering that I was most keen to relearn my English and the Japanese speech therapists didn't actually speak English. We spent most sessions forming sounds rather than words but I was already fairly comprehensible in day to day conversation. I had little control over tone or volume and I had to consciously flip between different mouth shapes to form multisyllabic words. I still caught my parents catching each other's eyes across my bed when I spoke sometimes – "Nope, me neither" – but less often than before.

Wanting to garnish my spastic Mancunian rocking out to the advert I launched into song accompanying the Gallagher's –

"I'mmm freeeee to do whaaatever " trilled Liam.

"Ermtreetoodowwitch...aver" was the stillborn mutant that tumbled awkwardly out of my mouth.

I sounded like a strangled cat. There was no force in my voice, trying to "sing" at the speed of the music was utterly beyond me, my voice ran out of breath in the middle of phrases and dropped to nothing.

I was mortified. I'd never thought this would be something I'd not be able to do anymore. I certainly wasn't a "singing is my life" type but I enjoyed a good singsong while I did the washing up and the odd night at the karaoke. It wasn't so much that singing was integral to my life. It was just another unexpected loss. It seemed as though I was losing things as quickly as I remembered I had them.

I broke down and howled. I'd cried so much recently that I was surprised that I had any liquid left in my body but, no, I still wanted to give a physical form to my anguish. Spluttering, gulping for air, I bawled. My whimpers filled the room. My dead arm shook involuntarily and my jaw juddered. Eventually I found myself again and lay back on the bed, sniffing away snot and getting my breath back.

Then she said it. It was said as a joke. Jun was attempting to leaven the mood with a bit of gentle ribbing. She said it in Japanese so my time-lapse mental translation took a while to catch up and allowed me to pretend I had misunderstood but, no, there it was –

"If I was you I wouldn't have cried so much"

I did cry loudly and histrionically most times Jun came to visit. I'm sure it was wearing and embarrassing to a member of a culture inclined to stoicism but, fuck! My life was ruined. I was mourning myself. What was I supposed to do?

How is the right way to have a massive, crippling stroke at 35? You're mentally preparing for that tough class at 3.15 when, without warning, your whole life changes monstrously for the worse, for ever. How do you take that in your stride? What do you do? How should you react? From that day I've always felt that I wasn't having a stroke "right". I felt as though I was letting Jun down somehow. She was disappointed in me. I'm tormented by loneliness and the feeling that there's no one else like me anywhere but, at the same time, other people would handle things differently – manage to take things on the chin more or bounce back quicker. I had no idea what was happening to me. Suddenly half of me doesn't work. Over the lonely months in hospital I begin to see that me and Jun react to things in very different ways. Bad news just confirms to Jun the essential evil nature of life. She always seemed to be half expecting it and as a consequence she coped better. I have a sense of entitlement and I hope that good things will happen. I couldn't (can't?) process this state of affairs. "This just isn't fair, why would this happen to me?" Jun often used to tell me that she thought the world would end in a few years. I didn't think she could be serious but after suffering my own personal apocalypse I'm not sure that anything can be relied on anymore. Her words haunt me still. Should I talk about it more? Should I talk about it less? Do I have the right to be depressed or am I supposed to roll out of my corner all guns blazing? Does my inability to move on and accept my new life indicate a flaw in my personality? Jun's not mean. She makes mistakes sometimes but she would never deliberately hurt me. Still it left me feeling that I couldn't even live out a nightmare in the right way.

Chapter 7

October 10th 2007 – 1 month since the crippling

Kaisei Hospital, Shin-Osaka, Osaka, Japan

The longer I stayed in the second hospital the more I liked the first one I was in. For reasons that I still don't quite understand I had to move hospital about 6 weeks after my stroke. As much as it is possible to feel affection towards a hospital that doesn't actually heal you I really liked Kaisei. It was modern and airy. There was the coffee place downstairs. The rehab room was huge and well equipped. We all seemed to approach the problem of "me" with vigour and optimism. I think everyone believed I was going to recover. They gave me extra, after-hours rehab sessions. The limits of my recovery weren't set yet. By the time I got into the last few months at the second hospital there was a detectable whiff of "best of a bad lot" about all our attitudes to my rehabilitation.

I didn't realise at the time but one of the nicest things about Kaisei was that it wasn't exclusively stroke patients around me. I wasn't even the youngest patient in my bedroom. I couldn't tell you what was wrong with him but he was young and tangibly improving day by day, attempting to chat up the nurses by night and sneaking out for fags in the day. This was one of the differences – the nurses weren't quite so conditioned to us. We weren't all "stroke survivors". The mixed nature of the ward meant that some people got better and left within the week while other people, like me, were more long term. I don't think that any medical staff consciously compartmentalise patients but, after a while, seeing too many of a similar type must colour your attitude toward them. "Oh, this is what happens to people with this kind of condition." Consequently the nurses here saw me as a bit more of an individual.

No, that's a lie. They saw me as a bit more of a gaijin than a stroke survivor. This meant marvelling at my ability to speak Japanese however mangled my talking still was and telling me with a conspiratorial wink that they loved "Pirates of the Caribbean" (being a white-faced gaijin meant that I obviously automatically loved anything with other white folks in. I remember one laboured conversation with a nurse where we struggled to remember the gaijin boy-band she liked. After 5 tortuous minutes we worked out that she meant Westlife. Then the rules of pleasant conversation dictated that I had to think of something polite to say about Westlife – a few awkward pauses in that conversation, eh?)

The nurses were all nice and kind and we had a laugh together especially after they got to know Jun and realised that she could be a bridge in the case of me not understanding something. Therapists made plans that I would teach them English when I left and nurses wanted tips on how to snag their very own gaijin bloke. Gaijin were thought to be much more gentlemanly and kind than a lot of Japanese men – no one had bothered to tell a lot of the white pigs I used to hang out with. I still thought I was going to get better so this was a kind of unusual working holiday. A lot of the nurses were pretty fit and their uniforms were an added bonus. Nobody flirted with me or was ever less than immaculately professional but I suspected I was a slightly more exciting stop on the daily round of blood-pressure taking and "number of pisses" interrogation.

I liked the attention. My self-esteem wasn't yet as shot as it soon would be and I felt like we were interacting on a level. Everyone at the hospital had just happened to catch me at an inconvenient moment or something. I was used to struggling through a day of lessons with the flu or the runs. Japanese people didn't really take sick days. This was really just a more extreme version of that. I liked to think that I was giving a little something back. Explaining to the nurse that we called "Kentucky Fried Chicken" "KFC" in England or that there was no such thing as "White Day"[4] at home. I had a fine time recommending gangster movies to one of my occupational therapists. All the stuff I hated doing in real life – showing off my supposedly huge nose, liking things just because they were made by a member of a similar ethnic group to me or gracefully accepting compliments about how good my Japanese was – I was happy to do here. In the real world I hated being "Gaijin Stereotype No.1" but here I was happy to play along. I liked to imagine that I was kind of unique – the first gaijin patient at the hospital? Maybe the first young gaijin stroke survivor in the history of the Japanese medical system? People used me as an example at study meetings and I think my photos are in a physiotherapy textbook over there. I felt that I was reciprocating a tiny bit. You've got to be grateful to the person that introduces you to "Goodfellas" for the first time,

[4] Valentine's Day in Japan is exclusively for women to give chocolate to men and White Day is the reverse when men give gifts on March 14th. There can be a romantic element to this gift giving but you are also supposed to give stuff to people such as colleagues etc.

surely? I still remember the person who was kind enough to give me my first listen of "Northern Sky" (Thanks, Janet!)

All the staff – nurses, therapists, doctors or orderlies – were kind to me. Except one. She was a female nurse. She had a name badge but I couldn't read the kanji that made up her name (unless you were Mr Mountain-Field or Ms River-Mouth or something equally simple I didn't have much luck) but she was large and ugly. She was rapidly heading towards middle-age. No wedding ring and a generally sour attitude spoke of a frustrated life. There's a tranche of Japanese womanhood whose ultimate ambition is marriage before thirty. She would have been closer to 40 by now and her wedding cake was well past its sell-by-date. She didn't like me. I think she thought that I came across as a bit full of myself. Perhaps I did. Perhaps I was still able to be like that back then. She would mock me in ways that didn't cross any guidelines about patient/nurse interaction but could be felt sure enough. Just slightly loaded questions or comments that fuelled my rising paranoia. "Again? I don't believe it!" when I called for the wee bottle for the third time of an evening. "What do your family think of you living here?" – seemingly implying that I had run away from home and stowed away in the cargo hold of a JAL jet. Or so it seemed to me. Maybe it was just that she was a bit older than a lot of the other nurses and less awestruck by my general whiteness.

I really should have perhaps not been quite so puffed up about being Garry Gaijin and just concentrated on being Sammy Stroke. Playing the exchange student allowed me to think about other things but it all crashed down on me towards the end of my stay at the first hospital. I loved telling everybody about Sai and one tea-time I was telling Nasty Nurse about him. I felt that she was affronted by my temerity in daring to take in a Japanese cat so I was really trying to prove what a responsible owner I was. We'd even taken in a kitten from a stray cat.

"A what?"

"A stray cat. Sai-chan's mum was a stray cat."

"Sorry, I don't understand. Psycho's mum was a *what*?" said with a seeming slight smirk this time.

By this point I can speak reasonably well and I know the Japanese for "stray cat" is "nara neko". I'm getting upset. All the weeks of playing nice with everyone and now she's deliberately not understanding me.

"Sai's mum is a **stray cat**. Don't you understand?"

I'm not saying anything rude or insulting but my voice is rising and my bad arm is shaking like mad. I drag a passing nurse into our row –

"**STRAY CAT! PLEASE EXPLAIN TO HER!**"

I'm fairly frantic to be understood by now. I don't care whether she knows about Sai or not but speaking Japanese is something I can do. I'm fucking good at Japanese. My wife is Japanese. We speak Japanese at home. I've taken and passed difficult exams. The other nurse doesn't understand either. I think she's just backing up her colleague so she doesn't lose face.

Saliva is flying everywhere. In normal life I sometimes have to concentrate to stop drool dripping from my open mouth but now it's arcing angrily away from my utterances, a physical counterpoint to my words. I don't think any of it actually lands on anyone but the viscous droplets are visible to all. My voice is getting higher and tighter. The nurses are getting calmer as I get wilder. This is the scary side of the gaijin. Shouting, out of control and wild-eyed. Not polite and restrained like Japanese people are. I'm usually repressed and polite. That's why I feel so at home in Japan. I don't talk about my feelings if I can help it. I'm English and male. I went to a rugby-playing private school where all that "feelings" stuff is frowned upon. This kind of thing exhausts me and always makes me feel horrifically guilty afterwards but this is too much to take. One of the few things that I've got left is my Japanese language skill and now my ability is being questioned. I can't walk, talk properly, dress myself, get out of bed or take a fucking shit. Now it seems like I can't even speak Japanese properly anymore. It's a step too far. I can't take anything else. I've accepted all this with as much good grace as I can muster. Until now. I wipe away spittle. As I rant more and more uncontrollably the nurse just gets calmer and calmer.

"I'm sorry I still don't understand. You should probably try to relax a little bit." Deliberate lack of reaction, reflecting all my anger straight back at me. It's a technique I understand well. I used to use it on 5 year olds with behavioural difficulties.

To make it worse I'm stuck here. I've been put in a chair at the table. The limited liberty of my wheelchair is out-of-reach on the other side of the room. I slump in my seat defeated and demoralised. I've lost my appetite, desperate to be back in my bed, curtains around me. Eventually they take me back. Everyone seems to steer clear of me for the next few days. Back in bed I consult the dictionary via my phone. I was wrong – "stray cat" is actually "nora neko" not "nara neko"[5]. I'm

---

[5]野良猫 – stray cat; alley cat

suitably chastened. I've been saying "stroy cat" the whole time. Retrospective shame courses through my body. My cheeks redden. I can't even do the things I think I still can. I see the nurse again the next day. It's all forced pleasantries and awkward silences. I'm sure I've reinforced all her prejudices in the same way I've reinforced those of the nurses I've been performing for. I feel a bit guilty for losing my temper but I don't apologise. "Stroy cat" to "stray cat" is not a mental leap beyond the realms of possibility, an unjumpable gorge of comprehension. Unless you don't really want to understand in the first place.

Chapter 8

October 5th 2007 – four weeks since the crippling

Kaisei Hospital, Shin-Osaka, Osaka, Japan

The first few weeks in hospital I really thought I was going to get better. This was just a game, something that would make a good story over nabe[6] come the winter. My father confidently assured me that he'd "done some research on the internet" and people usually made a full recovery. I wasn't slow in noticing than no therapists made any similar sounding promises. I'd taken a nasty tumble at futsal a few weeks before and my parents thought that was the cause. That had a nice "A causing B", "specific incident" kind of sense to it. Things are easier to understand if you can attribute them to a simple cause. It was a pretty spectacular, cart-wheeling, flying through the air and having time to think "this is going to hurt" before you hit the earth kind of fall. It was pretty bad but I had, naturally, exaggerated it exponentially in my weekly parental chat and I can see how some portentous significance could be attributed to it.

The doctor seemed a bit scared of me. His usual omnipotence somehow challenged by the fact I couldn't appreciate it. My Japanese

[6] A winter dish. A communal stew cooked on a little gas stove placed on the dining table. A very sociable way to eat.

was fine for day-to-day living – work interactions, chatting to pupils' parents, jousting with Jun – but I had zero medical vocabulary aside from "I think I'm catching a cold" and "How's your hay fever?". I sat in offices with Jun and peered pseudo-sagely at x-rays and M.R.I. images that were supposedly me. I could see a blob of white where there shouldn't be a blob but what it signified I had no idea. Jun tried to explain things in words that I understood but it still didn't make much sense.

It didn't really bother me too much that I didn't know what was going on in my body. Whatever had happened *had happened* and I didn't think there was anything that could turn it back. I tried to be confident about getting everything back but I didn't really believe myself. If my fingers didn't work now there wasn't really a sound logical argument that I could construct to say that they would or wouldn't start working again. Blind hope might work for some people but it was in short supply in my hospital bed. Me and Jun used to guess at what my physical condition would be by the time I finally left hospital. She, being a big fan of "House", went for stick user while I went for a wheelchair.

I wish it had been a conscious decision not to find out too much about my condition, some kind of "if I don't know what has happened to me then I can't let myself be defined by it" or some other kind self-affirmation credo but it was just that I wasn't good enough at Japanese. I should have hired a translator. I didn't care too much about the finer details but I would have liked to know why they had to inflict the existential terror of the M.R.I. on me again. For something that's so technologically advanced it sounds like nothing more impending medieval torture. I still don't understand how such an irregular, metal-on-metal clanking sound can result in a serene picture of a cross-section of my brain. It sounds like a device for shoeing a horse very quickly.

One word that I heard enough times to remember and think that I ought to maybe find out what it meant was - "のうこうそく". I'd heard this word enough that it stuck and I attempted a little research. "のう"? I knew that. "nou" meant "brain" and I had stared at enough pictures of my head in the last few weeks to guess that this was something to do with that. "こうそく" I had no idea about. "Kousoku" was a word I didn't think I had ever heard before. This attempt to piece together the meaning of an unknown word was a pretty familiar process. It was just something I did, idle commute-time curiosity. A desire to learn a language rather than to find out anything significant about myself. Still if the doctor was talking about a "brain something" in relation to me it had to have some relevance.

Phone in lap, I rolled my way up to the little alcove with the vending machines. I liked to be somewhere different to my bed and although it was a public space my white face normally scared off other punters. Sure enough, I was alone aside from the blinking buttons of the vending machine. I had subscribed to a dictionary, accessible from my phone. ¥500 a month for hours of ferreting around a language on the train to work seemed like a good deal. Firing it up, I inputted the characters and pressed the button to send my word to a server-bound database somewhere in a basement in Tokyo. Considering how this word would come to dominate my existence from that moment on, I didn't do any of this with any great ceremony. I remember opening the envelope containing the letter telling me that I hadn't got into Oxford. With teenage self-importance I'd made that more ritualised than Mass but this was nothing like that. I perhaps wondered idly which particular Lawsons snack food Jun would bring me that evening – American Dog or Nikuman[7]?

The mobile screen lit up, illuminating my face. I peered down. My vision still wasn't quite right and I had to give my eyes a few seconds to adjust their focal length –

"脳梗塞；脳硬塞；脳こうそく　【のうこうそく】 (n) stroke (blocked blood vessel in brain); cerebral infarction"

The words sat there, taunting me from the screen. As much as I wanted things to be different there didn't seem to be any getting around it. My eyes were in perfect focus now. I'd not made a mistake with my sometimes fat-fingered Japanese typing. FUCK! I didn't even know what some of the English meant. "Cerebral infarction" – what the fucking fuck does that mean? Strokes were something that old people had. I played futsal. I cycled most places. I wore Paul Smith shirts and Adidas trainers. I was planning to get tickets for Daft Punk. I'd never heard of anybody young having a stroke and I'd never heard of anyone getting better after one. My grandma had had a stroke when I was little. She was wheelchair-bound and barely spoke. She'd scared me, an alien presence immobile in the corner, a statue I was expected to venerate.

I'd been in here for not quite a month and I'd just found out what had happened. Somehow the discovery that I'd had a stroke didn't really shock me too much. The last few weeks had been so surreal that nothing could surprise me that much. I'd never really believed my family when they'd told me I was going to get better but now that feeling began to take root that much more insidiously. I knew that people had little strokes or big strokes but

---

[7] Steamed buns with a savoury filling in the middle.

no one ever seemed to recover, did they? I'd never heard anyone say "I was feeling a little stroke-y last week but I'm fine now"

The days and weeks dragged by. The flowers work had sent wilted in the vase by my bedside. My parents replaced them with some more until they, in turn, wilted, became brown and withered. Somewhere I stood alone on the futsal court, ball resting between hand and hip, that ineffably sad "golden hour" light flowing around me. No one comes to have a kickabout.

Chapter 9

October 11th 2007 - 5 weeks after the crippling

Kaisei Hospital, Shin-Osaka, Osaka, Japan.

I'm writhing and wriggling, a crippled salmon desperately trying to will himself upstream. This is face-reddeningly humiliating. I twist and convulse myself, a useless would-be contortionist. My exertions are compounded by my lack of dexterity and a clear understanding of how I should be doing this. I'm trying to move a piano by ear, sight read a score I don't actually possess. The rehab room is air-conditioned and airy, still beads of sweat prickle on my brow and begin to trickle down into my eyes.

My absolute inability is compounded by just how stupidly simple this is to everyone else. I look as though I'm fighting a monster made of light blue cloth or trying to scratch an itch in an inaccessible spot. My squirming embarrassment is compounded by my lack of motivation for the task in hand. I've rushed into every part of my rehab with a genuine wide-eyed enthusiasm, doing my utmost at whatever they've asked me to do. When enthusiastic physios have arrived late in the day offering me some extra sessions "if I'm not too tired" I've (metaphorically) jumped at the chance. I'm desperate to get better and this is the route I'm being lead down. They tell me I'll be in hospital for 6 months or so. That's a pretty long amount of time. Quite long enough to sort myself out. I'd seen enough films where protagonists made a full recovery long before they were actually allowed to leave the hospital. The last few weeks of lengthy hospital stays seemed to consist of crossword puzzles, ruminative pipes and flirting with nurses. Still I want to do everything they ask of me. I kind of think I'll just get better automatically (that's what people do in hospital, right? If they don't die they get better. No one seems particularly worried that I'm going to die any time now so, clearly, I'm going to get better. Simple logic. Just a matter of time.) but I'm eager to please all the same.

All the exercises and stretches have been done diligently. When they are trying to toilet train me I genuinely try, perched unsteadily on the toilet seat and straining unsuccessfully away. I knew that nothing would happen but I tried all the same. I've got no chance of squeezing anything out knowing that an attractive therapist is lurking outside the door ready to leap into the breech if I need any help with anything. I've dutifully used the washcloth Nishimura-sensei has made for me with the elastic strap so I can put my bad arm through the elastic loop and then hold the other end to scrub my back. She'd made it at home in her free time. I'm touched. I find out later that this is a common item and she could have just as easily ordered one out of a disability aids catalogue.

This, however, is the first time I've pulled up. Exercises help me to get better so I'd be daft not to do them. Toilet and shower stuff are needed right now – I can't do six months without taking a dump or a proper shower so it's only logical to learn this stuff even though I won't need any of it in a few months. But this? This doesn't make any sense to me. Why should I spend valuable rehab time wrestling with this ugly blue shirt before me? I've no need to wear a shirt while I'm here and then by the time I leave I'll be back to putting my shirts on like anybody else (a nice floral Paul Smith number, I should add, not this nasty salary man cast-off from the communal dressing up box). Nishimura-sensei has been very kind to me over the last few weeks so I want to play along but this is frustrating. I'm starting to heat up, my anger rising, blood boiling. I'm mad that I can't do something I don't even particularly want to do.

The mantra is always the same whether you're attempting to put something on your top or bottom – "bad bit first!". So I'm sat here trying to slide this shirt onto an immobile arm. My left arm doesn't move at all, aside from the shakes which are racing up and down my arm right now. Consequently it's like trying to dress a shop window dummy that's attached to you like the corpse of your Siamese twin. If you manage to snake it up your left arm then you have to try and wrap it round your back and then attempt to find the other sleeve hole somewhere behind you by touch alone and then slide your arm down. I feel like a reverse Harry Houdini.

Eventually I manage to get in and out of the shirt a few times and Nishimura-sensei is quietly exultant. She dives into the box of discarded clothes once more and pulls out a paisley mauve tie. It's horrible. I hardly ever wear a tie. The last time I put one on was when I got married. She ties it on and admires her handiwork. Let's out a little shriek of glee and calls another female therapist over to look at me. She claps her hands together and tells me how cute I look. We've left therapy behind and now they're playing with their very own dress up gaijin, crippled Ken with no Barbie in sight. After a while Nishimura-sensei remembers her job and fetches a full-length mirror. I look myself up and down and manage a weak joke about how I could be going for an interview at Tokyo University. Oversize shirt hanging awkwardly over my new, asymmetric body, the thin end of the tie far too long, thick end conversely too short and glasses slanting on my nose. I've never looked less like myself. Again I wonder why I've just spent the best part of an hour learning a skill I'll never need. I'm exhausted, irritable and rehab has finished for the day, no extra sessions in the deserted, echoey room tonight.

Two years later I'm still dressing the way Nishimura-sensei taught me that afternoon. My arm is slightly more mobile now but still no actual help in getting stuff on. I'm forced to think of Nishimura-sensei every morning as I dress – trying to match the right hole to an inert arm. I still get things wrong when I'm in a rush – T-shirts end up back to front and hands poke stupidly out of neck holes. Still I always get there in the end and I'm glad that Nishimura-sensei taught me so patiently. I hated it at the time and hate having to still do it now but the steps she showed me allow me to start my days with the minimum of fuss.

Summer's coming and I order a t-shirt on-line. It comes with a freebie button badge. "I dress myself" it reads, black childlike characters on a white background. I pin it on my jacket, wearing it with what hopefully seems like ironic pride. It is a joke but I do want people to know. I can at least do *that* much.

Chapter 10

October 18th 2007 – 6 weeks after the crippling

Kaisei Hospital, Shin-Osaka, Osaka, Japan.

It was time to change hospitals and I was scared. The concept of moving had been raised a few weeks ago but it had seemed to rush into view much too quickly. I'd barely got slightly used to this place before it was the day to move hospitals and the wheelchair taxi was due at 9am that morning. I didn't understand why I was moving but I then I didn't understand anything these days. I have no ownership of my own life any more. The hospital is in a place called Kawanishi. I've never been there before.

Nishimura-sensei arrives at my bed just after breakfast to say goodbye. She takes a photo of us together and gives me an envelope addressed to "Mr Matthew". I opened it and read through. It's written in decent English. Nishimura-sensei is interested in the world outside of Japan and has travelled a bit around Asia but I the last few weeks have shown that she can't speak much English. I wonder how she has managed to write this letter. She explains – she had got a friend who was studying English at university to translate her Japanese into English and then dictate it laboriously back to her down the phone line. I was touched. At the bottom of her letter by her name and email address she had cut out and stuck a happy looking face from another sheet of paper. A "1" Is printed under the face. I recognise where it has come from and laugh genuinely and ruefully. I've seen that simply drawn, ridiculously happy face pretty much daily for the last few weeks.

At the end of every physio session (except those when I was gushing blood) Nishimura-sensei would finish by pulling a crinkled piece of A5 out of her pocket. On it were 20 simple smiley faces of varying degrees of happiness or sadness. "1", the face she has glued at the bottom of the letter, was a face of ecstatic gurning rapture while "20" was a suicidal grimace. In-between was every variant of line drawn smiley face possible – upturned grins, jagged lips, welcoming eye-shapes and diagonal lines of frustration. Drips of angry sweat flew from foreheads and bemused question marks hung above hairlines. The question for me was "which of these coin-sized pictures adequately express your state of mind?", "Which particular slanting angle of nose exactly represents your feelings of panic and horror at this precise moment?"

I knew things were bad. I was in hospital and half my body didn't work for fuck's sake but I didn't really know just how bad things were on a scale of 1-20. In my heart of hearts I suspected this was a "20" but this all still felt like a game. This wasn't really happening to me somehow. It clearly wasn't a dream but things had a hallucinogenic quality that saved me from the full terror just yet. Still if this was how my life was going to be from now on then it was clearly a "20". I was worried though that going in with a bullet at 20 would consign me to some kind of suicide watch and my sleep would be continually interrupted by nurses checking up on me on the hour. Trying to find an answer that said to everyone that I was coping but not deluded, I plumped for "15". Hopefully that made me sad and scared enough to be believable but not *too* sad and scared. During the course of my stay I would adjust my smiley face up or down by one depending on how things seemed to be going – some days I was “14”, on others it was “16”. This was the only time until I tearfully staggered into my English GP’s office 10 months later that anyone asked me about my mental state. Nishimura-sensei was trying to tell me that I would, one day, get to “1” but I doubt her ambitious prediction is ever going to happen. She is the only health professional who has ever made anything like a promise about anything relating to my stroke. Whether “1” relates to my body or my mental health I’m never going to reach it. A really good day is maybe an “8”. Me and my counsellor agree that things are always going to be some degree of bad. I have to be realistic. Life is always going to be hard. I don’t resent Nishimura-sensei for an unfulfilled promise. I thank her for her hopes.

Part 2

Chapter 11

May 10th 2004 – 3 years 4 months until the crippling

Nakatsu, Osaka, Japan

I unashamedly work on Jun. I spend a full week convincing her that if her allergies are too bad we can get rid of the cat.

"If it's too bad we'll just send him back to your mum."

"Let's just try and see how it goes."

"Maybe you'll get used to it over time?"

I'm relentless, working gradually towards the erosion of opposition. The thing is – I believe myself when I spout this stuff. I genuinely think that we can get rid of the kitten at any point in the first few weeks. Just send it back to Jun's family and wash the moulted fur off our hands. Walk away scot-free. Take the ill-fitting shirt back to the shop. That's how I think I'll feel until Sai tumbles out of the cat carrier and onto our kitchen floor. I've never felt such immediate, unequivocal love for anything. I adore him with a passion and a desperation that surprises me. I can't quite believe that this little thing depends on us for his safety and well-being. He doesn't really, he's from stray cat stock so he probably has an innate survival instinct, but he does as much as anything ever has so far in our lives.

Obayashi, where Jun's parents live, is a bit more rural than where we are. There are hills, gardens and little bits of unused ground here and there, overgrown and brambly. In one of these next door to Jun's mum's house a heavily pregnant stray cat has taken to appearing. Over the next few weeks Jun's mum, Suzuko-san, looks out for her daily appearances, prepares the sardines and milk in readiness, marvels at the cat's ever expanding stomach. She notices when the cat doesn't turn up for a few days. Eventually a weak, mewing sound from under the house alerts Suzuko-san to what has happened. A week or so later the new mum reappears with 4 tiny ginger balls of fur in tow. These kittens were in no way her responsibility but she took them in, let Mum rest and syringe-fed the babies. She is a kind person who likes a "project".

Me and Jun had vaguely discussed getting a cat. I cynically saw it as a child dry run. See if I could cope with the responsibility before maybe moving on to more demanding endeavours, an advanced kind of flour baby. It was an aspect of "grown up" that I thought I could perhaps cope with. Jun was dubious because of her allergies. She was worried that a cat in the house would lead her to permanently itchy eyes and a non-stop runny nose. We periodically debated. I wanted a cat. Jun didn't particularly. It was a momentary disappointment to me but no more and soon enough the conversation moved on to what we were going to have for breakfast the next day or where we were going to go on holiday next – Vietnam or Bali? The cat ownership issue would have remained little more than idle banter if a litter of kittens hadn't dropped on Suzuko-san's door step. We would never have gone to the pet shop and chosen one ourselves. It was the unplanned but welcome surprise pregnancy of pet ownership.

As soon as Jun told me about the kittens she must have known we were going to end up getting one. It's testament to her good nature that she even told me. A little judicious non-disclosure would have been much simpler. She put up some valiant, if futile, protests before conceding with dignity and agreeing to snatch a kitten from the group in a few days. Despite our absolute lack of any kind of feline knowledge aside from "they're cute" we prepared as best we could – a water bowl, a food dish, a scratch board and a litter tray were all placed on sheets of newspaper against a wall in the kitchen. Jun bought him home on the train in a cat box on Friday night, patiently responded to my need for a running text commentary of the journey. I needed to consider every aspect of the little guy's comfort.

"We're at Nishinomiya-Kitaguchi. He's OK but a bit noisy."

"Kanzakigawa now. He's fine."

"Yes, we're at Juso. He's still fine."

I was on tenterhooks, jiggling by the door until she and him finally arrived. I could see that Jun was determined to be as non-committal as I was carried away but I didn't really care. She came in the door, laid the cat carrier on the floor, put her own bag in the corner and leant down to undo the clasps on the door of the container. Out slithered a ginger ball of panic. This tiny kitten, no bigger than my hand, looked around in abject fear and dashed to the nearest safe looking place. In the case of our little kitchen this meant "behind the fridge". Much to our chagrin, there he stayed for the next few days amid the fallen grains of rice and spilt sesame seeds. Eventually a desire for food and a lessening of his terror drew him out and he began to interact with us.

Thankfully Jun's allergies receded so he could stay. He is a beautiful, mischievous cat as lazy as he is naughty. Through the stages of his growing up he's remained as beautiful as the day he arrived. His coat is every shade of ginger that there is – auburn, ginger, tawny, brass, flame, apricot and every gradation between. He's a walking Pantone chart of orange. When he was "perched on shoulder" small he was basically a pair of eyes on legs, forever widening as he tries to take everything in – just how much fun you can have with a cereal box and why there are whitebait cascading through the letter box. As he grew older he became a little fat but no more complacent – fighting with the cat two doors down or hiding in next door's house and refusing to leave (he must have been able to smell the source of the magically appearing white bait that same neighbour posted through the door).

Jun left naming duties to me and I called him "Psycho" after the Nottingham Forest legend. Luckily a similar sounding word[8] means "the best" in Japanese so it kind of worked in both languages. Anyway he was barely ever called his given name, most of the time he was "Sai-chan" or "Sai-kun" or "Psychedelico" or some similar bastardisation. Jun got up three hours before me so she usually went to bed equally early. Often I would browse the internet or watch telly on my own with Sai perched comfortingly on my lap, my patented antidote to loneliness. I felt as though I'd invented human/feline cohabitation and Sai was the first domesticated animal in the world. He was surely the most beautiful cat ever. I could project anything onto his lethargy and simple desire for warmth. Conversely, in our central-heating free home he is a valuable source of winter heat. He's always happy to see you home from work, usually so keen to tactilely connect that he'll jump on

---

[8] 最高 - saikou

you when you're halfway through your tea or daydreaming part-dressed on the bed. Jun is quite happy to unceremoniously chuck him off her lap. I reluctantly do it but it breaks my heart. We soon learn to keep the TV remote within arm's reach at all times. The wide-eyed look of reproach as you turf Sai off you to stretch for it is shaming in the extreme. Soon enough he'll climb back on board you and hum himself to sleep.

Sai is my mate. He's clearly bilingual – he ignore us equally well in English or Japanese. He was my buddy during long nights of watching time-difference English football. As night drifted into morning he'd be weighty and reassuring in my lap. As comforting and demarking of "home" as the Lisn Autumn Twilight Incense stick I would burn later. Jun's allergies wouldn't allow him to sleep with us so we'd shut him in the downstairs when we went to bed. He hated it, not so much sad to be separated from us but more amazed that we would think we had the right to deny certain areas of the house to him. Unfortunately paper fusama sliding doors are no match for a meaty cat and his pointy claws. We had a few nights of Sai just clawing a hole in the door paper, coming in and waking us up at 4am, a feline Jack Nicholson in "The Shining". Either that or he'd just paw the door across and open. Jun, that much closer to getting up time, would lose her rag (this was when I learnt the Japanese for "I've fucking had enough.") until we hit on a solution. We used a battered Orson Welles biography that was just the right size to jam between the side of the door and a set of shelves next to it. The muscliest cat couldn't slide the door open now. He could still claw holes in the paper though. That was quite scary. Suddenly waking bleary eyed and finding the cat looking at you with silent scorn – "The door is shut: Sai was the other side of it a moment ago now he's sat on my chest. What kind of 4am sorcery is this?!" We finally cured our night terrors by taping some of the laminated A4 picture cards I used to teach the kids vocab at kindergarten on to the door. These particular cards were used to teach jobs. The plastic covering was too smooth for kitty claws to penetrate. From then on fire-fighters and ballerinas kept silent guard while we slept.

I was in hospital so long they let me home for a few weekends towards the end of my stay. I think the idea was to help me readjust to being outside the ward again. My biggest fear was that Sai would have forgotten me. I rolled towards my house full of trepidation. As I opened the front door and negotiated the tricky step up from the genkan[9] Sai rushed towards me and wound himself dangerously between my legs. He looked happy. Later on as I dozed on the tatami he leapt onto my borrowed wheelchair, got going with his satisfied purr and contentedly fell asleep. He remembered me. He's forgotten me now but, back then, he remembered his daddy. For a moment it was enough.

---

[9] 玄関– small porch at the entrance to most Japanese houses. A place to change out of your outdoor shoes and into indoor slippers. We just took off our shoes and wore our socks. In our house you had to take a big step up from it into the body of the house. A really difficult step when you're not used to doing them anymore and there are no handrails.

Chapter 12

March 10th 2007 - 6 months until the crippling

Obayashi, Hyogo Prefecture, Japan

The train clanked into the station and we got off. A Junior High School baseball team was waiting to take our place. A small branch line station, the platform was quiet, virtually deserted aside from the budding sportsmen. The station was carved into the side of a hill. The ground on the right hand side was much higher than the ground to the left. The station exits were at very different heights depending on which side you left from. We were heading down the hill but if your intended destination was uphill you needed a flight of stairs and then the bridge over the tracks.

We left the station, Jun simply waved her credit card in the direction of the wicket and the gates opened by magic (her credit card company was part of the train company so her train tickets were bought by the card and included in her monthly statement. I didn't quite understand how it worked but Jun saved a bit of money somehow and no money or tickets being involved presumably increased efficiency for the train company. Plus it looked *really* cool when you rocked up to the ticket gates and did no more than waft your wallet in the vague direction of a sensor to be let through. God! I fucking love Japan!) I put my prepaid card in the ticket machine and retrieved it after the saloon-style gates had let me through.

Not as "I live in the future" cool, I grant you, but free. Jun's parents run a dry cleaners. You'd be amazed how many people would leave half used pre-pay train ticket cards in the pocket of trousers to be cleaned. "Left in trousers" clearly meant "forgotten" to Suzuko-san and she would fish them out and pass them on to me to help lessen the cost of my commutes. I had a slightly queasy feeling about the whole process but it was a moral grey area – could it really be stealing if the owner wasn't even aware that he had lost anything? Well, "yes" by pretty much all ethical frames of reference but there was often a lot of yen left on those cards. The fact that I was at least compromising myself for a decent amount of money, often as much as the equivalent of £17, made me feel better somehow.

We trot down the hill. It's only 100 yards to, their shop, Adachi Fashion Cleaning, but I take the opportunity of a hot can of coffee from one of the many machines we pass. I quite enjoy my yakiniku[10] evenings with the in-laws but it tests my language skills to the limit. I need all the stimulants I can acquire.

We go inside the shop. Jun's dad, Isao-san, is behind the counter changing his trousers – trackie bottoms for the steamy work in the shop but a proper pair of slacks for a night out. I love checking out the shop – huge industrial iron, motorised racks to hang the clothes on and whirr them round to you, various machines too steampunk and arcane for me to even understand what they do. There's even a machine to put those polythene sheets over the clean clothes.

---

[10]焼き肉- strips of meat that you cook yourself over a grill in the centre of the table. It's a sociable sharing way to eat. If you ate out you would rarely order a dish for your own specific consumption. Most restaurant meals are made up of many smaller dishes that are communally shared by everyone.

We exchange greetings and Isao-san drives us the short distance to the restaurant. We go in and the waitress leads us to our raised tatami mats. We sit on the mats around a table with the grill built in. The waitress brings us raw strips of beef and we use chopsticks to grill them ourselves. Turning them until both sides are just so and eating them with dipping sauces and rice. Yakiniku is easy enough to understand for foreigners. No whale or baby squid or sparrow or anything. Get beef, cook beef on the grill in front of you, eat. It was tasty and there was little opportunity to commit a faux pas. I'd been in too many "the flowers look lovely but am I supposed to eat them?" kind of situations so I was grateful for a meal which didn't blur the boundaries between "stuffing your face" and "culinary artwork" too much.

Jun's family are not used to talking to non-native speakers and I struggle to follow too much of the conversation, especially when they are talking among themselves. After Isao-san has had a few beers he likes to practice his English on me – "Hello", "How are you?", My name is Adachi Isao..no, no! Isao Adachi". I feign being impressed and hope no one notices my insincerity. These evenings are a bit of a trial for me, trying to understand and wanting to be understood, not wanting to cause offence, wanting to show some of the real me but not wanting to disagree too much with anyone. It's unfortunate that their family dynamic, as many are worldwide, seems to be based on arguing, complaining, and piss-taking. One easy way to endear myself to them is to "comically" complain about Jun. So that's what I do but afterwards I feel cheap and tawdry. These events never lasted much past 8.30 but I was always exhausted by the time I got home.

The thing is - I really want Jun's parents to like me. I want them to trust me, to think their daughter is in safe hands. Not that I think they care so much about Jun's well being. Life's vicissitudes – divorce, theft, repossessions and an ever desperate struggle to keep the family finances above water – has left them with little excess emotional energy to think about anyone but themselves. Or to pay too much mind to the social niceties.

I moved in with Jun three months after we met. Unmarried cohabitation is not unheard of in Japan nowadays but to live together quite so soon and with someone quite so non-Japanese was a big deal. Isao-san was admirably sanguine towards me – laying eyes on me for the first time as he carted Jun's possessions into our new home. After I proposed to Jun I found out that I was expected to visit her parents and formally ask their permission to marry. This is supposed to be quite a significant occasion and I took it seriously. Earnestly getting Jun to teach me the correct formal Japanese for the situation, digging out my rarely-worn suit and getting it cleaned at somewhere that wasn't Adachi Fashion Cleaning. The Sunday morning of the big visit came. I polished my shoes, shooed the cat off my vaguely pristine suit and debated appropriate omiyage[11] with Jun. Her parents knew what I was planning to do, the visit was expected, the result foregone, but I wanted to impress them with my appropriate behaviour. Being whitey was not an excuse anymore, not if I was going to make a permanent life with Jun. I took Japanese stuff seriously.

[11] Ritualised gifts given in Japan. Pretty much required in any situation – after a holiday or day trip, on the first day at work and after being given a present. It's a complicated and serious process.

The phone rang just as we were preparing to leave. It was Jun's dad – the dog was moulting. Tell "Matto" not to bother with suit. No point creating more work for themselves. They would feel obliged to dry-clean my suit if it got dog hair on. I quickly changed out of my suit and into "me" clothes and immediately felt ten times better. We went. I garbled my way through the set phrases and they gave their blessings. Isao-san was probably more embarrassed than me, struggling to resist the urge to laugh at my awkward kneeling and ill-timed bowing. They were great towards me. Certainly kinder than I expected after hearing other horror stories from other Western potential partners.

The first time we had gone for yakiniku Isao-san had tried to freak me out by getting a bulb of garlic, having it wrapped in foil and then grilling it at the table. I think he expected me to struggle with the heat of the garlic but, to his slight disappointment, I had thought it was delicious. Since then it had become the special treat he bestowed upon me. It wasn't on the menu but he always demanded a bulb wrapped in tinfoil. He grilled it at the table and we bonded over it. An all-male treat the ladies couldn't hack.

Pores sweating meat, we eventually left. Much as we tried, guilty in the knowledge that we had more disposable income than them, Isao-san and Suzuko-san would never let us pay. Isao-san would drop us off at the station but we'd sneak back into town to explore the discount chemist's and raid the local ¥100 shop.

On the train home I was dog-tired and Jun seemed quietly relieved that imagined social disasters from either side had been averted once more. Back in Nakatsu we hit the nearest convenience store for reward drinks – chu-hai[12] for Jun, Yebisu beer for me. Jun was in bed by 10.30. I settled down on the sofa, can in hand. I was enjoying a carefree drink for the first time that evening unconcerned my linguistic skills would be damaged or my alertness and concentration would slip.

Jun rolled over in bed and let out a sigh. I set a stick of Autumn Twilight in the holder ready for my bleary eyed tumble into bed in a few hours. Collapsing on the sofa I reached for the remote. Psycho jumped into my lap and made himself comfortable. A long night of time-difference Premiership football lay ahead of me.

---

[12]チューハイ – a kind of Japanese alcopop

Chapter 13

July 7th 2007 – 2 months and 9 days to the crippling

Tennoji, Osaka, Japan

The train rattles into the underground station. The rolling sound of the wheels echoed round the underground chamber. The platform wasn't too busy this morning so I was able to walk along the platform a little as the train pulled in and scan the carriages. No sign of Euan yet. He lived further up the Midosuji line so we would try to meet on the train heading down to Tennoji and the futsal courts. His station was on the same line as me a few stops away. The idea was that he would get his train and then I would spot him from the platform as he rode through my station, jump aboard and join him. This plan was great in theory but in reality it failed as often as it worked. Either I missed him completely as he sailed through my station or even when I fluked the right train I couldn't find his carriage. This tricky process was further complicated by poor underground mobile signals, my neurotic desire to never be late for *anything* and Euan's expansive social life that often made 12.30 on Sunday a faintly tricky proposition.

The train rolled out. Consumers of all ages bound for their retail fixes – Namba Parks, OPA, Daimaru, Takashimaya, Loft or HEP 5. I found a bench and settled into my MP3 player – Vashti Bunyan sounding pastoral and bucolic but perhaps not ideal as mobile locker room music. The next train rumbles in after a song and a half. I manage to spot Euan and join him in the carriage. He looks tired and greasy. He needs a shower. He's probably not been to bed yet. I'm so glad I met Jun. I don't miss the nightlife. The Midoduji line is one of the city's arteries connecting Umeda to Namba to Shinsaibashi and Tennoji. Shoppers flock to these areas at the weekend. They're the West End, the Oxford Street of Osaka. The other passengers all look smart – Manga hair, Louis Vuitton and desirable phones. Me and Euan are in our football kit and stand out even more than we usually do. Two gaijin, a head taller than most people around us, kitted out in a hodgepodge of mismatching football togs. We're pretty conspicuous among the fashion conscious. I'm sporting Birkenstocks with a pair of nasty white Umbro football trainers in my oversize bag, a "Winning Eleven United" Adidas shirt indicates my loyalty to virtual football even as I endeavour to do the real thing. My bag is stuffed with three or four thin towels ready to be strategically positioned to soak up the inevitable gallons of sweat. Euan is better prepared. His towel is already tied bandana-like across his forehead and over his scalp.

My bag sits awkwardly across my back. It's huge, not designed for crowded train carriages. White vinyl Adidas, it's probably three foot by two. It's the kind favoured by High School baseball teams who clog up trains on the weekend laden with equipment – bats, mitts, catcher's masks. It was a present from Jun and I treasure it. Not for it being particularly useful, if anything it's a bit too cavernous, but because it's a little bit of Jun with me there.

The train pulls into Tennoji. It's primarily a shopping and business district. My company has offices there and I occasionally bump into my Japanese colleagues on the way to squeeze a little more unpaid overtime into the week. When I see them there's a momentary feeling of guilt but I always stress that I'm off to play futsal with my Japanese friends and I figure they like to see me integrating. Me and Euan exit the station and its attendant inevitable shopping centre and emerge, blinking, into the daylight. The futsal courts are a few hundred yards down the road, waste ground entrepreneurially made into cheap courts and portacabin changing rooms until bigwigs decide which particular exciting shopping or dining opportunity they're are going to share with us.

The heat is predictably astonishing. It must be knocking 40° and the sun beats relentlessly down. Parasols seem mandatory for girls. Nobody would contemplate walking around with their shirt off over here but shorts are worn by most men under 40. Sweat is pouring from every pore already. Exercise and exertion will simply justify it. I lathered myself in sun protection before I left the house and will do periodically through the rest of the day but the sun seems able to worm its way into any unprotected patch or crevice. Over the years here I've had sunburnt ankles, peeling earlobes and tender elbows. The sun is a blanket of potential pain and the heat is stifling. Perhaps the natives are a little more used to it but I find it unbearable. I pretty much spend four months of the year indoors, only leaving the house when I have no other choice, rushing from one air-conditioned building to the other.

But this is different. Even on the most brow-beatingly ridiculously hot day I still turn out with my fellow Calamari. My team had been christened "Calamaro" after a complex mobile phone voting procedure. Apparently this was to do with a squid having 10 "legs" and so did the five men on our team. We would become one creature like a squid, 10 appendages but just one brain. We often played like we didn't actually have one brain between us. I didn't really get it but I liked it because it made me think that were going to all suddenly squelch and become a giant squid, an unstoppable footballing kaiju[13]. We'd become as terrifying as we were skilful. The simple lung-bursting joy of these afternoons is priceless to me. All my stress, money worries, anxiety about my future simply disappears for those two hours. I want to win and become frustrated when I lose but, above all, I love the kinetic, pin-balling energy of playing with the ball. I love the ludicrous improbability of the moment the ball hits the net. There are an infinite number of ways that a sequence of passes can go wrong. They very often do but there's a moment, maybe only once an afternoon, when everything goes perfectly and everybody manages to do exactly what they intended to do and what they intended to do is exactly the right decision for that moment. You're on the beach and your pile of sand suddenly becomes a pinnacled Disney palace. I love how the desire to do well and not let any of your team-mates down removes the capacity for any non-related thoughts from your head. I love that it's Shankly socialism in action and I love how terrible my muscles feel afterwards. We had managed to win a tournament one day a few months ago and it had meant *something*. Afterwards we had gone for a Chinese Buffet with a genuine sense of achievement. We weren't just a bunch of middle aged men with very little common ground aside from our beginner's paunches. We were slightly over-weight, unfit men with very little in common who had won a little plastic trophy. It felt great.

Futsal was ideal for us. Originally developed in Brazil to encourage close control in youngsters, it was played with a smaller ball and the

[13]怪獣– Japanese monster – Godzilla or Mothra, perhaps?

artificial pitch was not much bigger than a tennis court. As great as it was for kids it was also great for older gentlemen who couldn't get around the pitch as well as they once could. And weren't actually all that great at football to begin with. To be fair some of our players were pretty good – Nakamura-san, Moriguchi-san but there were plenty of us who were inept but enthusiastic. I don't really understand how the team was put together and what all the connections between people were. We'd heard about it from Makoto-kun who we'd played with in another team.

I can't pretend I knew anybody very well but it was nice to meet people in a different context. Me and Euan got to know these people because we all liked football. That made a very refreshing change. In Japan I'd found it hard to get to know anybody Japanese who wasn't looking to meet a foreigner to either practice or learn English. That was my u.s.p. – I spoke English and I was a novelty. These guys had no desire to meet a foreigner. Hashimoto-san didn't want to practice his English. Aoki-san didn't want to show me off to his friends. We all liked playing football. Being gaijin was a bonus to them, something unexpected to explore but it wasn't the defining point of the relationship. I can't pretend I understood everything that was said but I understood enough. We shot the shit, took the piss out of each other and laughed a lot.

The stopwatch hit the appointed time. Our last game was over. With weary limbs we raked the thin layer of sand over the artificial turf, poked carpet burns inquisitively and drained sports drinks. I called Jun and got her to run me the bath with the expensive herbal tablets in. Me and Euan trudged towards the underground laughing about the day's incidents. The train was less crowded now. Sated shoppers clutched newly-acquired purchases. Me and Euan probably smelt rank, sweat-soaked hair congealed to our foreheads- “henna gaijin na!” [14]

I rang Jun to doublecheck that the bath was ready. It was. It was stupendous.

---

[14] 変な外人な！- Strange Westerners, eh!

Chapter 14

August 21st 2007 – 16 days to crippling

Okinawa, Japan

We're at Okinawa Airport waiting for our flight back to Osaka. I love airports. The expensive shops selling nothing you would ever need or buy under normal circumstances but somehow because you're so limited in choice *anything* available becomes desirable. Jun called her mum from the departure lounge while I pondered if my life would be any different if I owned a pair of Gucci sunglasses or a Louis Vuitton man bag.

We were tired but content. Jun had her travel bug sated for a few months. We'd perhaps struggle to afford our Christmas trip to England in a few months but we'd manage somehow. We always did. We were supposedly saving up for our future life in England but it wasn't working out too well. I'd tried to look stern and say we couldn't afford a summer holiday this year. I'd managed to stay firm for a week or two but Jun seemed really down and distant with her Moyamoya so I inevitably crumbled. We compromised – no luxurious foreign holidays this time. We'd stay in Japan. Okinawa was about as foreign as Japan got.

Even with the rushing and lugging involved in getting back home we were criminally relaxed, still in absolute holiday mode. I went to

Starbucks and got us coffee. It was called “coffee” or “strawberry mocha frapuccino” at least but there didn’t seem to have been much contact with any beans – vanilla cream, strawberry syrup and chocolate sprinkles on top. It was ridiculously self-indulgent. A week of calories in a cup. I think we had three, laughing at cream spots on our noses and the slurping sounds we made as we tried to hoover up the last globules of flavour among the melting ice.

It had been a wonderful holiday. Okinawa really wasn’t like Japan. Taxi drivers stopped to show you wild flowers by the side of the road and even I could spot how different and sing-song the native accent was compared to the harsh sounds of the mainland. We’d canoed in a mangrove swamp, island-hopped and cycled round deserted lanes. We’d crossed a river in a cart pulled by a water buffalo, paddled in the sea on a deserted beach and survived tornado warnings. Me and Jun sat side by side in the Departure Lounge, full of love and Starbucks sugar rush. I smiled at Jun and she smiled back. Mrs Padmore – I’d never been that bothered about getting married. I’d always been content to live with Jun but, at this precise moment, I was glad we had done it. I felt legitimate and grown-up. Me and my wife on holiday in Okinawa. Mr and Mrs Padmore. I smiled a furtive smile, amazed that I had managed to pull this all off. Jun looked at me quizzically before joining in, my quiet joy infectious.

Jun has that enviable Japanese trait of being able to fall asleep anywhere at any time and she settled down for a snooze. I wandered aimlessly around the islands of chairs. Scattered about the room were four or five large screen TV’s on little tables at the end of rows positioned for maximum visibility. Behind these TV’s were floor to ceiling windows allowing you to watch things on the apron and the runway – take-offs and landings, boardings and exits, passengers and baggage. A plane caught my eye. It was stationary on the tarmac with nobody boarding or getting off. It was a decent size commercial plane, tagged "China Airlines". Mostly white it had a blossoming flower of some kind on the tail fin. The entrance door was open but there where wasn't one of those motorised stair ways parked up linking it to the ground. Instead a thin grey plume of smoke snuck out of the door and inched up into the sky.

That wasn't right, surely? Was I the only person noticing this? Slowly a small crowd of aghast onlookers gathered by the window staring on to the runway. We gawped and gasped but nothing seemed to be happening outside.

The plume grew bigger and blacker, filling the doorway in its rush to be free. We could see flames dancing behind the passenger windows now. I didn't know if there was anyone on the plane – a stranded cleaning crew collecting unread in-flight magazines for minimum wage perhaps? – but I couldn't stop looking all the same. Eventually, after what seemed far too long, fire trucks arrived sirens blazing. Fire-helmeted figures began to scurry around, dousing the plane with foam.

Unhappy about losing my prime viewing spot, I rushed off to find Jun curled up in her chair. Shaking her awake, I gesticulated towards the smoking plane, full of rubber-necking joy and puppy dog eager to share. Jun reluctantly roused herself. I pointed towards the runway. Flames could be seen flickering through the tiny gaps that the onlookers left, between legs and under armpits.

We shuffled through the crowds to try to find somewhere to watch from. Inevitably my spot had been swallowed up but I noticed the TV's were showing footage of the fire live on the lunchtime news. The camera must have been on top of the room we were in. The images were pretty much what we could see out of the window. The camera seemed to be limited in its movements, just a sweep of the area. I guessed that the TV broadcast was just using the airport's CCTV footage direct. We watched tiny firemen pointing hoses towards the fuselage and more and more fire trucks entering the scene. Beyond the TV we could just see, between the shoulders' of spectators, the real scene unfolding before us but we preferred to watch the TV screen. Even with my limited Japanese I could tell that the reporter putting a voice to the images didn't know any more about what was going on than we did but we still watched the screen, hypnotised. Things seemed somehow realer on the little screen. We stood side by side in silence as the plane finally gave up its struggle and the body broke in two, both ends collapsing onto the concrete. We watched the telly as the flames danced and the foam arced.

No one died. The plane had been empty when the fire started. We eventually got back, delayed and nerve jangled. For once not minding how late we were. We were just happy to be home and safe. The holiday had been wonderful but the burning plane and the potential for tragedy was the abiding memory of that week. It was the first thing we told our friends about and the last thing we saw when we turned out the light at the end of the day.

Chapter 15

September 5th 2007 - 24 hours to the crippling

Nakatsu, Osaka, Japan

I wake to the sound of the alarm on Jun's phone. 4.30 am. Usually I manage a brief chat with Jun before she disappears for the day. She does a couple of hours ironing at her parents' dry cleaners, 6-8am, before she goes off to her real job formulating dyes at the underwear factory. Her parents are perennially on the brink of financial disaster and they can't afford to pay for any help so Jun chips in. I generally feel momentarily guilty as Jun empties her side of the bed at 4.30am but it soon passes and I turn over back into my duvet and pillow and a few more hours fitful sleep.

I'm never quite relaxed enough first thing in the morning and, as much as I don't want to get up, I'm always awake before my alarm goes off. Being late for anything is a terrifying prospect for me. I drag myself out of bed and into my dressing gown. Through the summer months we just leave the air-con on the whole time we are in the house so it's not too hot. I head downstairs and set the coffee machine going. Just two cups worth – enough to last me until I go to work. Next I feed Sai – third of a can of pet food, some dry kibble and fresh water. I've already showered the night before so all I do is clean my teeth and wash my hair. Loads of deodorant but no aftershave. I always wear some at the weekend but I won't wear it at work. When I first qualified and taught in a tough secondary school in Sheffield I used to put some on but the uncomfortable experience of 15 year old girls telling me leeringly how nice I smelt made me soon give up.

Back upstairs I got dressed then went down again for the first of my two essential cups of coffee and my first internet sweep of the day - email, football, news and auction sites. It would take me about half an hour to get through everything and then I would have to do it all again when I got back from work.

Second cup of coffee downed, I left the house and headed to my first school of the day. Mornings were full kindergarten classes and the afternoon was smaller, optional, paid for classes. Today was Kusunoki Kindergarten – modern, well-run and thankfully not too far away. I taught three 40 minute classes to a bunch of five year olds. I liked it there. The proper teachers were friendly and involved and the kids were easy to manage while still having a personality. I was supposedly teaching "English" but it was really not much more than "having fun in English". I'd start the lessons with a song, get everyone to say hello to me individually and give me a high five, we'd look at some picture cards and practise some vocabulary and then use that vocabulary to play a simple game. End with a song to say goodbye. Keep it bubbly and loud, shower everyone with praise and compliment the form teacher about how great her kids were then leave and go to the next classroom and do exactly the same thing again. It seemed to me like it was something that a trained chimp could do but I enjoyed it all the same and I was good at it.

Lessons done there I headed back to the station. I'd had Wednesday afternoons off until recently. Sorry, I'd spent Wednesday afternoons "preparing new teaching materials and reflecting on my practice" until recently but I'd been co-opted into my company's latest innovation. We had expanded into doing English lessons at a temple as opposed to the usual kindergarten. It wasn't going well. We had no captive pool to fish in and those promo posters round the neighbourhood soon became faded and tatty. I never had more than two kids for any lesson and the front bit of a temple was not a great place to attempt to control kids. I spent my preparation time desperately trying to put exciting things out of reach of little hands. And it was miles away from Osaka – almost in Kyoto and far too far from the nearest station.

The subway brought me back into the main Osaka station. I nipped into a nearby bakery and grabbed stuff for lunch. Bought my ticket, rode the escalator up to the platform and waited in the metallic heat. My stop was Mukomachi, far too far away but long enough for me to eat my pastries and get some decent MP3 player time in – Super Furry Animals' "Love Kraft" today, I think. The journey was long, the station was small so only clanky and slow local trains stopped there. We'd often stop at stations for a few minutes to allow faster trains to pass us by. I was about the longest serving passenger by the time I reached my destination. Waves of passengers got on and got off a few stops later while I bided my time and nodded off to sprawling psychedelia. Everybody in motion except me.

When we finally reached the anonymous dreariness of Mukomachi the next part of my odyssey began. The temple being too far away to walk they had arranged to leave a fold up bike for me in the front yard of a friendly temple worshipper who lived across the road from the station. I would retrieve said bike, call my formal greetings out loud and clear toward the residence, never seeing a human once in my all my time there, and cycle to the temple. This was easier said than done. The bike was tiny, my bag was huge and heavy, crammed full of all the pictures, rewards and general gimcracks required of a day of bringing the Anglophone love to the kids. The temple was a good 10 minutes away and I would wobble and sway my way there, arriving sweaty and dishevelled on hot days. Rainy days were worse. Once there I would unsuccessfully attempt to teach lessons. Class sizes were so small that I'm sure the fees the parents paid barely covered my wages. Even tiny kids, after a month or two of kindy, understand that a classroom is a place intended for study and a certain standard of behaviour is required. You'd think that the behaviour would be even more reverent in a place of worship but seemingly not. I think the juxtaposition of "super traditional Japanese place" and "super non-Japanese guy" just kind of short-circuited their systems. That and the fact that with so few kids in the classes there often wasn't actually anybody doing what they were supposed to be doing. Usually there would be five or so "good" kids demonstrating to the "bad" kid how they were supposed to behave. Here, with the class sizes so small, terrible behaviour was the norm. The only voice of authority was that weird looking and sounding gaijin over there. I was easy to ignore. I was in Japan nearly eight years and this was the worst behaviour I ever encountered. Or at least it seemed that way because the surroundings seemed so precious – statues, golden fixtures, ornate carvings and ceremonial incense burners. If racing kids damaged anything it was only ever going to be one person's fault - "That lumbering barbarian doesn't respect anything". I was scared of hurting anything sacred and it all seemed sacred to me. What if that dusty white board mouldering in the corner had some deep religious significance I wasn't aware of? The lessons suffered for it.

When the kids weren't stressing me out it was a serene place. The resident priest rarely bothered me and I was able to relax on the three or four steps leading up to the interior and enjoy my surroundings. The smell of incense lingered in the air. Echoes of earlier ceremonies or just the mosquito coil thoughtfully lit prior to my arrival? The little garden in front of the temple was all rock and moss gently taunting me, a coded message that I wasn't enlightened enough to read. I had no idea how old this little temple was but the worn-smooth wood beneath my socks felt warm and dependable. I had few opportunities but if ever I got a little bit of peace and quiet while I was there then I would begin to be infused with a waft of serenity. It almost made it worthwhile going.

The final lesson of the day was over and I gathered my stuff, keen on a quick getaway. More formal phrases of thanks volleyed towards an inanimate building and I got going. Bike was returned and train boarded. Terry Callier cooed me home. This time I had to change onto the subway at Shin-Osaka and I took advantage of the big station facilities to get some sweet waffles for the evening. This was my longest workday of the week and it was gone 7 by the time I got home. Jun had got ishiyaki-bibimba[15] ready for as soon as I got in. We ate together and laughed about all the weirdos we worked with. None of them had any idea about "ningen kankei"[16]. Most of my workplace human interaction was with 4 year olds but the basic principle still applied. She had her bath and went to bed early as she usually did. I stayed up later. Maybe I watched a DVD. I think I was still working my way through "The Sopranos" box sets around that time. I had a slight

[15] Korean rice and vegetable dish served in special heavy stone bowls.
[16] 人間関係 – human relations, a basic idea of how to treat staff and colleagues.

headache but it had been a long day. No need for any aspirin. I poured myself a glass of “The Macallan”. Drank it, checked my e-mail one last time, brushed my teeth and headed up to bed.

Stripped down to boxers I wriggled under the duvet, careful not to disturb Jun. Without wanting to manhandle her too much I gently kissed and nuzzled the back of her neck. She didn’t wake up. My last movement of the day, as it was on any day, was fishing an Autumn Twilight joss stick out of the packet, fixing it in its holder, lighting it and switching the light off. The smouldering light of the stick glowed gently and the musky fragrance wafted about the room. I was asleep before it burned out.

Part 3

Chapter 16

November 7th 2007 - 2 months since the crippling

Dainikyouritsu Hospital, Kawanishi, Hyogo, Japan

Walking shouldn't be this hard, surely? After the age of 2 you just do it. One foot in front of the other, left, right, left. It just happens. Unless you are impersonating a soldier or a robot it just happens without any conscious effort and before you know it you're running, jumping, hopping and dancing.

So why can't I do it? I want to do it but I'm scared that I can't. There are so many things I'm supposed to remember – distribute your weight evenly between both legs, bend your left knee as much as you can, look forward towards the horizon and don't stare at your feet. These are just the ones I'm remembering today. Everything has to be taken in, mentally translated into English from the therapist's original Japanese and then remembered. The problem is that walking is scary. I'm usually clinging so desperately onto the arm rails that all I can manage to focus on are my fingernails attempting to gouge handholds into the wood. Depending on quite how terrified I am at a particular moment the toes on my gammy foot curl under and attempt to grip the smooth parquet flooring. Then we have to stop and let me calm down. Me and Yamamoto-sensei walk up and down a route marked off by two handrails about three feet apart. Doing the stretch in-between the two hand rails feels secure and contained but the journey back, outside the secure zone, with only a handrail at my right and the oceanic expanse of the rest of the rehab room to my left is head-spinningly scary.

My left foot and all the toes have no conscious movement in them. They'll move but not because I want them to. My left knee bends a little but extremely slowly and not without focussed thought. The biggest problem is the shaking. Not just in my leg but in my arm and, most disturbingly, my jaw. Exert any undue pressure on my leg, tire it out, try to get it do anything it doesn't want or think mean things about it then the tremors start. Just as often they'll start for no apparent reason just to remind you not to get cocky. Imagine a Force 9 earthquake centred on a San Andreas Fault running down your leg. It's pretty disturbing to have absolutely no control of parts of your body. These shakes course down the whole of my leg, toe to hip, great convulsing masses of alien uselessness, good for nothing, not even part of me. Leg highways, knee amphitheatres and toe tower blocks all collapsing and crumbling to dust. All I can do is stop whatever I'm doing and marvel at the treachery of my body. The shakes will often die down after a minute or two – mission accomplished. Walk aborted, rehab session abruptly truncated or misplaced outburst of fledgling self-esteem crushed

My days are spent in constant calculation – current walking ability versus time left in the hospital. They've told me that I will stay in hospital for about 6 months and so I have to be walking perfectly by then. It's a sliding scale. Sometimes I feel that I'm ahead of schedule – they were walking me round the rehab room, three therapists manning limbs and working me like a marionette, at three weeks after my stroke but other times I feel the sand in the egg timer running by all too quick. Two months before I leave, two/thirds of the way through my time, I'm still walking up and down the tramline bars. I never walk much more than, say, 100 yards over an hour session but I'm exhausted come the end. After a rehab session is one of my designated canned coffee times. I head up to the telephone corner where all the vending machines live and telephone use is allowed. I grab a coffee, check my email on my mobile and stare out of the window into the car park, marvelling at people doing things with no thought. Things I can only dream of.

Walking is only ever done downstairs in the rehab room, never for anything useful. It's just walking as a concept, something to aspire to. Any meaningful travel was done in my wheelchair – bed to dining table, bed to toilet, bed to rehab room. I didn't have a stick until a week before I left so even if I had possessed the ability to walk I couldn't have freestyled it. Only my right hand worked so they couldn't even try me with a walking frame. How I envied those guys who came in with two working arms. A couple of weeks and they'd be rocking up to dinner on their own two feet, parking their walkers under the table next to them. God! I hated those smug fuckers! Everybody got better quicker than me – people admitted after me and released, fully functioning, back into the wild before me.

I never really understood how it did or didn't work. I and everyone around me just assumed that the more rehabilitation you did the better you got. They checked your blood pressure before you started your physio session. Too high and it wasn't deemed safe to carry on with physical activities. One day my blood pressure was over the limit and they had to send me back, crestfallen, to my bed. No rehab for me. I was in tears – denied a chance to get better. When my arm shakes started, uncontrollable spasms shuddering down my arm, mocking my inability to move it myself, Jun greeted them with joy. "Oh, hello!" The way she saw it the shakes showed that life was still there. I tried to believe her but that's not how it felt.

My ambitions retreated over the horizon. I couldn't help thinking about the toddlers I was used to seeing everyday at work. They hadn't been able to walk and then they just could. The work of a few weeks. What was wrong with me?

By the time it came to leave I could walk unaided maybe 50 yards. Yamamoto-sensei never left my side. The thought of walking anywhere alone terrified me. I had walked exclusively on the smooth, flat wooden floor of the rehab room. Slopes and any kind of different textures on the floor were never involved. The only outside walking I'd done so far was the couple of yards from taxi doors to house doors and vice versa on the couple of weekends I'd been let home. I hadn't fallen yet and so was scared stupid at what would happen if I did. Perhaps it would have been better to allow me to do it once or twice at the hospital so I'd that while it was plenty mortifying it wasn't the end of the world and I could just about pick myself up from the floor. We'd worked hard, me and the various physios, and I had got a bit better. I could now walk a short distance but it felt like a party piece rather than anything day-to-day useful. I was better than I had been before but I was much, much worse than most everybody else.

I'd always sworn to myself that I would walk out of the hospital even if that meant no more than negotiating the sliding doors at the entrance on my feet. In the end such attempts at bravado just seemed token in the extreme. I could probably have managed those ten yards from the sliding doors to the taxi. Perhaps. Just. But what was the point, really? Who was I fooling? It would have been meaningless contract fulfilment, the live album of my recuperation. Instead Jun juggled the plastic bags containing the meagre possessions from my temporary home and I let the nurse push my wheelchair out of the doors and towards the waiting car.

Chapter 11

December 6th 2007 - 3 months since the crippling

Dainikyouritsu Hospital, Kawanishi, Hyogo, Japan

I go to Speech Therapy everyday. This must be the hardest thing to do with me for the therapists. Bodies are all the same, we all walk in a pretty similar way. You can't recognise someone's nationality by their walk. As long as I understand what they're saying there's no real problem with trying to fix my leg. Aside from all the problems *with* my leg. My speech therapists are entrusted with teaching me something that they don't know. None of them speak English. They can find lip shapes and tongue positions that I'll need in English and we can practice but they'll have very little idea if I'm getting them right. I did want to get my Japanese back but English was my native tongue. However proud I was of my Japanese I still thought in English 99% of the time. When I spoke any kind of sentence in Japanese it was always formulated in English and then mentally translated before I tried it in Japanese. I occasionally caught myself thinking in Japanese but that was only for very simple exclamation-mark kind of utterances. I needed my English back. That was my first language.

I don't really know how the stroke has affected my mouth. For a few weeks after the stroke I'm not allowed to eat on my own, therapists staring intently at my mastication. My swallowing is a concern and they give me special easy to swallow jelly drinks. They have also decided that, as a gaijin, I will clearly like sliced bread rather than rolls. Every mealtime I get two thick slices of dry bread and not enough butter to spread on them. Dry bread is difficult to get down when your saliva production isn't too steady, you're being diligently observed and you have run out of drink.

I sound blasé but my speech basically just comes back over a number of weeks and months. The speech therapists give me opportunities to speak, record my voice so I can listen to it – the most humiliating answer phone message ever. They give me exercises and my speech does get clearer over the months. I have very little volume left. We record my shouts and measure the decibels. They improve over time but it's still nothing worthy of the word "shout". Subsequent times when I lose my temper the volume of my voice misrepresents the depth of my emotion – expressions of heart-rending traumas emerge as mild irritation, the heinous decimation of my whole life sounding like a minor annoyance over a missed train . My biggest problem is a lack of breath causing the abrupt curtailment of a speech mid-sentence. This followed by a diver's gulp for air and a stagger to the end of the line, all momentum lost.

"Jun, I think we should probably...(startled gasp, awkward pause, infinite possibilities hang unuttered in the air, Jun shuffles closer to my bed)...think about getting a can of coffee"

Over time I start to learn to time my breathing better and get to the end of my discourse uninterrupted. Either that or just learnt to speak in shorter sentences. I speak much slower than I did before and it sounds like a dirgey monotone. As a teacher, I loved the ear penetrating power of my voice. It had a little bit of drama, beguilingly quiet when it needed to be or loud and booming when I feigned anger or demanded attention. An old girlfriend use to tell me how much she loved the sound of my voice, begging me to sing/speak her to sleep. Now I could communicate reasonably well but there was no joy in my voice.

As my speaking improves there's not a whole heap that the speech therapists can do with me. I move from reading random encyclopaedia passages to children's picture books to "His Dark Materials". I read 100 pages of it aloud, the therapist uncomprehending and daydreamy in our 30 minute sessions. We tried some sessions practising Japanese but my Japanese, while comprehensible, was so idiosyncratic and jerry-built that he was basically having to teach me from scratch. Japanese is a pitch accent?

I'm obviously much younger than a typical stroke survivor so there was a lot of theorising about me going back to work. It seemed ludicrous to me that I could run a class with half a body and a half a voice but everyone was keen for me to give it a try. To this end the therapist arranged for me to teach an English lesson for interested staff and patients. I really didn't want to do it. I would have preferred just to be able to concentrate on being me before I started performing for anybody else but I usually found the path of least resistance easiest to walk and this was another example. A date was set for the "lesson".

As much as I didn't want to do it, this was my bread and butter. This is what I did – dragging unwilling, nervous speakers through an English lesson. Who cared if they remembered a word afterwards? They had spoken some English! The only difference this time was that the age of the students was different and, oh, I had lost the use of half my body since I had last done this. I talked through the lesson with Watanabe-sensei, the speech therapist. I managed to whittle him down to 20 minutes of lesson time but there was no getting out of it. We didn't know how many people would come and if they came how many people would want to join in or just gawp at whitey. Patients were so bored that they would do most things – the daily wheelchair aerobics sessions were always full. I didn't want people to expect anything but I hoped a decent crowd would appear. Large groups make time pass quicker and, for some reason, it's easier to ignore 50 eyeballs trained expectantly on you than it is to ignore four.

The day and hour came. We commandeered the dining room and shooed the habitual T.V. viewers away. Watanabe-sensei tried to get them to stay and join in but they were having none of it. I was planning to do a simple ball toss/self introduction thing. I teach everyone a few simple phrases, they practice the phrases and insert their own details. I randomly chuck the ball from person to person and they say the phrase. Everybody speaks and everyone goes home happy. "Jiko shoukai" [17] is a big deal in Japan and always a good topic for a one-off lesson. The dining room seemed cavernous. A room for fifty completely empty save for a few giggling nurses. Slowly wheelchairs rolled ominously in, walking frames clacked across the floor. Very few people arrived on time. It was twenty minutes past time when we started. I should have been finished by then. Still I can do this. I know how to do this. I've been a teacher for over ten years. Some things

---

[17] 自己紹介– self introduction. An essential part of the induction process in any Japanese group activity. It's kind of the verbal equivalent of your business card.

change but some things never do. I take a deep breath and start – "HELLO! EVERYBODY! HOW! ARE! YOU! TODAY!"

It's an unmitigated disaster. The phrases I write on the whiteboard are illegible. My voice won't carry in this size of room. Someone finds a microphone. Juggling the ball, the microphone and the board marker is impossible. In my wheelchair I have no presence. People at the back can barely see me. I can't throw a football-sized ball properly with one-hand. Surprisingly recovering stroke survivors don't make great catchers. Nurses spend a disproportionate amount of lesson time scurrying under tables to fetch balls that have bounced of faces. I demand that people who haven't uttered a word in any language in months or years speak in English. There was a lot of frantic head shaking by nurses stood behind particular patients. Soon the lesson plan I had meticulously written out on a bit of paper lies on the floor, crumpled by my frantic wheelchair to and froing. Another victim of my awkward one handedness. I tried to bring everyone together and end things on a united, positive note. "Firm lesson beginnings and endings" I'd always been taught all those years and miles ago. There was very little crowd left. Most of the patients had slunk away kindly trying to ignore my disaster. The nurses and physios had no choice but to stay. As I croaked an ending the physios quietly slipped away and the nurses seemed relieved to get their room back and to be able to start arranging the tables and chairs for dinner time.

Watanabe-sensei smiled a wan smile, thanked me for my hard work in achingly ritualised Japanese and snuck away. This afternoon was supposed to be the beginning of a series of English lessons, one-a-fortnight for the duration of my stay, another triumphant step on my road to rehabilitation. No more were ever scheduled. I think everyone was glad.

Chapter 18

December 31st 2007 – 4 months and 3 weeks since the crippling

Nakatsu, Osaka, Japan

Towards the end of my hospital stay they let me go home for the weekend a couple of times. It's exciting but somehow even more alienating than being in the hospital. At the hospital it's sort of understandable – I don't recognise where I am but that makes a strange kind of sense seeing as I don't recognise myself anymore. Now, here in the place I know best in the world, everything is familiar except me. It's disconcerting in the extreme. Jun is the same as she ever was. So is Sai. The downstairs living room is still scattered with Jun's discarded clothes. The computer is the same as is the litter tray. My mountain bike is propped up outside. Everything is identical but me. Somehow being at the location of my old life shows me just how distant it is now. I feel like I'm going to a museum. I'm also scared to go back to the place I had my stroke. I hope the vomit stains on the tatami have faded.

Before they can let me free from the hospital there are instructions to heed and routines to practice. Their major concern is getting up. I can't get upstairs and downstairs we have no chairs so I'll spend most of the time on the floor but if I ever need to get up for anything – to go to the fridge or the toilet – I'll have to get up from the floor. Me and the physios spent a lot of time in the pretend house practising various techniques. The one we settled one was a complicated process requiring order and concentration. It was like trying to learn to drive yourself. I'd try to plant my right hand firmly down on the floor and push up as far as I could on that. From there I would attempt to jump my left leg as far under my torso as I could manage. There was little upward thrust to come from here but it was an important stabilising strut in the arm/legs tripod I was creating. At this point I looked like an old-time sprinter on his blocks waiting for the starter's pistol – right leg with knee to foot resting on the ground, left foot on the ground and left knee at 90°. My right hand claws the ground, desperate to pump. My left arm dangles uselessly in front ruining the sprinters pose. At the signal, the starter's gun for the sprinter or an unignorable order from my bladder, we'd be off. Arms thrusting and legs pumping, he would race down the track. Arm thrusting and leg pumping I would wobble up to the vertical. I think I collapsed downwards, once or twice but, on the whole it worked ok.

From there I would grab the door frame and pigeon step it to the kitchen and my wheelchair. I didn't trust myself to do *anything* yet. It had only been a few months ago that I'd had to learn how to shit again. I couldn't possibly expect myself to walk 15 feet across a kitchen. So that was where the wheelchair was positioned. I would gingerly cross the living room and then, at the threshold to the kitchen, make a graceless pirouette before slumping into the welcoming embrace of the wheelchair. Then I'd turn the wheelchair round through 180° and roll across the kitchen. At the door to the toilet I would get up again and walk to the bowl bracing myself against the wall. I didn't trust myself to wee standing up so I did everything sat down. I was terrified of having to rush to the toilet and falling over in my haste so the slightest tingle in my pants sent me pre-emptively across the kitchen. I would often have to go (or think I needed to) a few times during the night. It was hard squeezing around a sleeping Jun. I didn't want to wake her but I was scared about falling over so, in a way, I did want to wake her in case I got into trouble. I spent a lot of time on the toilet *just in case*. From filling the coffee machine to writing an e-mail I just assumed I wouldn't be able to do it. No "I'll have a go and I'll probably work something out as I go along". I didn't think I could do anything anymore aside from crying. I would have got Jun to breathe for me if I could.

Inevitably I was in the toilet when the phone call came through. My jogging bottoms pooled around my ankles as I idly eavesdropped on Jun's call. By the formal tone of Jun's Japanese I could tell that she was talking to someone in authority. She knocked on the door, came in and passed the phone to me. Hardly anybody knew I was here. Who could this possibly be? I was still pretty unsure that I would even be understood on the phone.

"Hello Mr Padmore, this is Planetsafe, your health insurance company."

It was a young, female voice with an Antipodean accent. My insurance company had offices in New Zealand. Today was New Year's Eve. I was surprised that anyone was working anywhere especially not in New Zealand. It was tea-time here but it must have been well into party time over there. Health Insurance is a legal requirement in Japan. When I'd first arrived it was on a government exchange scheme so they sorted out all the formalities. Then after I finished on that I had bumbled through a few months of bitty part-time jobs and overall skintness. I hadn't sorted out any insurance. I knew conceptually I was breaking the law but I never seemed to get sick and had other "setting up home" priorities for my limited supplies of cash. Still when I got a new job and the managers offered to enrol me in their company-recommended insurance policy and charge me for it out of my wages I was very happy. Another step towards being a proper grown up. The company seemed decent and my managers seemed to trust them. I trusted my managers.

I don't know who had aligned the planets in the beginning to ensure that hospital bills were paid. I was too busy in my coma to notice but it seemed that the hospital, my employers and the insurance company were working in harmony. This was a small glow in the darkness, at least none of this was costing me anything. I was even kind of making a profit. I doubted the monthly premiums I had barely noticed going out of wages would even begin to cover the cost of even one M.R.I. scan. I'd had loads of tests, scans and rehab sessions. It must be costing a fortune but this was something I'd prepared for. Done the right thing. I was covered. Hospital bills seemed to be being paid and I didn't want for anything. I looked quizzically at the phone. I didn't really understand what they could want on New Year's Eve. That was a holiday, right?

"Mr Padmore? Your illness has been reclassified. It is now "chronic" and as such we are not liable for your hospital costs. We will honour your medical bills until 1st of January 2008 and then they are your responsibility."

All this tumbled down the line in one gulp as though the speaker just wanted to get it all out. I was silent for a couple of moments as I unpicked what had been said. I was unused to having a conversation with another native English speaker. Finally I worked out what was being said. I understood the words but still not the import. I asked her to explain again even as horrific realisation began to creep over me.

“Mr Padmore? Our latest medical reports indicate your condition is now “chronic” and, as such, is not covered by Planetsafe. Please refer to your policy document. Any hospital bills you incur up to today will be paid by us and then they are your responsibility.”

I was in shock. My arm, my leg and my jaw were all shaking. As unfair as all this seemed it was somehow right as well. My world was collapsing around me on a daily basis. This was just another aspect. What would my Dad do in this kind of situation? I tried.

“I’d like to speak to a manager, please”

“Ok, Mr Padmore, please hold.”

The tears are rolling down my face. I’m hyperventilating. Panic and anger are rising up my body. My head is getting hotter. My pants are still on the floor. My dick is a pathetic addendum.

“Mr Padmore, I’m sorry but all the managers are at the New Year’s party. There’s no one above me to talk to. I’m sorry.”

I’ve lost control completely. I’m screaming down the phone.

“**I want someone to call me back as soon as possible. You fucking people have ruined my life. Do you realise that? I’m dead! I’m fucking dead!**”

I'm torn. I'm raging. I'm terrified and I need to yell at someone but this woman at the other end of the phone is not directly to blame. She sounds young, early twenties. She works for an evil company but she probably isn't evil herself. It sounds like she's been set up to do the dirty work while the bosses are conveniently not present and won't be around for a few days. I'm just snuffling and crying down the line now. I think she might be as well. I'm getting nowhere and I can't trust myself to form intelligible words anymore. I hang up and hang my head.

I go back into the living room and try to explain what has happened to Jun. I don't really understand myself and I can't really explain in Japanese. I'm due to stay in hospital for two more months. This is the last push to sort myself out. I still can't walk unsupported. My left arm and hand have no conscious movement. I'm starting to fear that I'm not actually going to recover but, all the same, I have to give myself the best possible chance. I've got work to do. I don't know what each day at the hospital is costing me but I'm pretty sure it's a fortune – bed, board, rehab sessions, none of it will be cheap. Japanese hospitals are run as businesses.

The next few weeks are the worst I've ever experienced. I debate not going back to the hospital. I'm totally unable to comprehend how my life, any life, is going to carry on after the stroke. I don't understand what I can possibly do for the rest of my life. And now with the added prospect of millions of yen of debt and no obvious way to earn any money. I go back to hospital but am terrified that somebody is going to suddenly appear at my bedside and chuck me out onto the street. I'm in a constant state of terrible anxiety. Will the insurers contact the hospital? Will the next bedside visitor be telling me to pack my bags?

Might that be the best thing anyway? Save me running up mountains of debt? I had three rehab sessions per weekday and then the occasional Saturday bonus. Everything was absolutely essential to improve me physically just as everything came at a price and seemed like it was going to drag me further into an inescapable pool of debt. When the hospital did find out what was going on they were very understanding. That was an advantage of being a weird foreigner – they didn't expect anything involving me to be straightforward. They offered to cancel rehab until everything was sorted out but, really, what was the point of being there if I didn't actually do the rehab? I wasn't going to get better just lying in bed and eating nutritionally-balanced meals.

Gradually things become slightly clearer. I had no idea what it meant to be "chronic" but that word seemed to be what the situation hinged on. Turns out that it means no one thinks I'm going to get better and I'm going to be like this for ever. As unlikely as it seemed with every passing day, I still hoped I was going to get 100% better so this wasn't great to hear. I would have assumed this would have kicked me into some higher category of cover but it actually meant that the insurance company wanted to wash their hands of you as soon as possible. The prospect of huge, ongoing medical bills didn't have much appeal to them surprisingly. The fact that I and every other policy holder were paying our premiums with the assumption that we would be protected in precisely this kind of situation didn't seem to bother them. "Comprehensive" health insurance that doesn't want to cover you when you are properly sick seems as though it isn't really that useful. My parents kindly offered to pay my remaining hospital bills. This was going to run into tens of thousands of pounds. They could probably afford it but it would put a serious crimp in their retirement plans. My life was irreparably fucked up but I didn't want to ruin anybody else's. I would have taken the money, of course, if I had to but I would have felt *really* guilty. We also explored getting me included on Jun's national health insurance. Even though I hadn't paid any contributions for years apparently I was eligible as I was now officially Jun's husband. This would mean that 70% of my medical bills would be covered. This sounded a little better but 30% of "loads of fucking money" is still "far too much money really".

My parents were great about arguing with high-ups and sending bolshy e-mails to various people. There was talk of involving MP's, newspapers and, even, Anne Robinson. Frantic texts winged their way between Japan and England. Eventually they managed to find some small print they could argue over and the insurance company agreed to cough up an extra $15000 towards my bills Who was right and who was wrong, how much of the insurance company's softening stance was p.r. and how much was caused by fear of a genuine legal beatdown or whether we should've held out for more cash I neither knew nor cared. It was something to hang on to. Something that meant I could sleep safe in my bed again. Me and Jun sat down with the nice hospital administrator and worked out exactly how many more nights that would cover. It worked out to be just about enough. I came home in the middle of February, M.R.I films tucked under my arm. I'd spent nearly 6 months in hospital. I never heard from the hospital or the insurance company ever again so I assume that everything was OK. Being back in Britain would be terrible in a million ways but one undeniably wonderful thing was the N.H.S. I dove gratefully back into the arms of a universal health care system and there I've been held safely ever since.

Part 4

Chapter 19

March 1st 2003 - 3 years and 7 months until the crippling

Kobe, Hyogo, Japan

I first met Jun in Kobe. It was terrifying to meet a stranger at the station. I'd bought a new denim jacket for the occasion, wanting to impress. Jun had introduced herself as a "fashion designer" and I was as intimidated as I was intrigued. I'd self-consciously bought this Levis jacket to wear. You can't go wrong with a denim jacket, can you?

I needn't have worried. Right away I felt comfortable with Jun. She was friendly and fun, kind-eyed and pretty. Normal like I thought I was normal. She was the least intimidating fashion designer I could imagine. Her hair was resolutely symmetrical and her clothes seemed to work as clothes. They didn't seem to be trying to make a comment about anything. She told me her favourite label was Hysteric Glamour. We spent the morning in the "Hyogo Prefectural Museum of Art" looking at an exhibition of British Victorian paintings. The location and event was carefully chosen by me to show just how "sensitive" and "cultured" I was. It was as boring as hell. Portentous rain clouds seemed to dominate every canvas but thankfully Jun bore with me and afterwards we were saying our goodbyes when we both seemed to agree to stop pretending we had anything more exciting to do with the rest of the day. After a little awkward "Well if you haven't got another appointment we could maybe...you know, if you're not too busy...I'm quite hungry..." to-and-froing we agreed to go to Chinatown for an all-you-can-eat buffet lunch. This was much more our cup of tea. We both stuffed our faces and managed all the "getting to know you" stuff without too much awkwardness. We went our separate ways after lunch, reasonable first impressions seemingly made on both sides and definite plans hatched to meet up again soon.

I'd first got to know Jun over the internet. 32, lonely and a little desperate I'd placed a personal ad in a local, free English language magazine. I'd had relationships since I'd been in Japan but nothing had stuck, either they were too nice or too scared that I'd given them AIDS or there was too much Xanax hidden in their handbag. I wasn't meeting anybody socially and was reluctantly starting to resign myself to the single life. The ad was a last spin of the roulette wheel. I had drafted something that attempted to portray me as achingly cool. I think I mentioned Nick Drake and Cornelius among other supposed hipster touchstones. The odd reply drifted into my inbox over the next few weeks but it was all a bit tepid. I imagined there were from the kind of people who would just send a ready-written letter to any advert that appeared. I wasn't proud enough not to reply but nothing had seemed worth pursuing. I'm sure my co-correspondents felt the same.

Jun's letter was different. I'm sure mine wasn't the only personal ad she'd ever replied to but her email was personal, engaged and engaging. Our correspondence carried on for a few weeks and it began to be the highpoint of my day. I would rush home as quick as I could to check for a new message and then compose my reply in my head at work all the next day. I remember when we finally got to the photo sharing stage of things I held my breath in worried anticipation as I clicked on the attachment. Luckily Jun was lovely. Smiley and pretty without being unapproachable. She was at a temple festival with her friends but instead of doing anything devout she was eating takoyaki[18] and wearing a black with shiny silver bits woolly hat that I later grew to love.

We set a second date in Kyoto a week or two later. I chose the restaurant. "Merry Island" was near to my house, had a Balinese fishing canoe as the centrepiece of its decor and was boho and informal enough not to send out any confusing signals. Things were complicated by the fact that Jun lived with her parents out towards Takarazuka, a good hour on the train from me in Kyoto. As great as Japanese public transport can be it stops over night like anywhere else. The last train was about 11pm. I hoped she'd somehow end up missing the train but didn't want pressure myself into having to make a move. Nothing would be worse than making a rejected move and then Jun having to stay over anyway. Boy! Would that be awkward! I had to respect my general romantic ineptitude. I booked the table for early doors.

We had a wonderful time. The food was great – tofu in sesame sauce, pork mince sandwiched in white radish slices. We got on really well – all that stupid, superficial stuff that the beginnings of relationships are built on – we both liked being cold rather than hot and didn't like London that much. I was drinking carefully. Enough to bolster my faltering courage but hopefully not enough to become a slobbering perv. Jun just drank. Whisky straight up. She wasn't hugely drunk but the last train time passed, seemingly unnoticed by her and silently but

---

[18] たこ焼き - Fried, octopus, dumplings. An Osaka speciality. Usually sold from market stalls or fast food vans.

triumphantly celebrated by me. Where could we go after but back to my one room apartment? I kind of knew what was expected next but didn't have a clue how to achieve it. Luckily Jun had her hair up. Two explosive buns on the back of her head, elaborately held together with pins. Two black starbursts. Her hair sprayed out in all directions like the flowering split second of a firework. Frozen in time, the moment before each individual burst of light separates from its companions and begins to tumble earthwards. As she settled onto my sofa she began to unpick herself. I took the opportunity to "help". Sat with her back to me I began my work. With each hairpin I removed I planted a gentle kiss on the small of Jun's back. This is how it began. Now the fireworks were mine.

One last thing I had to do, didn't want to do but really had to. As much as it felt like too much too soon, like all the conditionals required to make my point might not carry in English or Japanese.

"Jun," I reluctantly came up for air, "Jun, listen!"

She looked at me expectantly.

I gabbled it out – "Jun, I'm going back to England one day. Probably not for a few years but I am going to go one day. If we were still together you could come with me if you wanted but I'm going to go one day." I felt stupid saying this then. It was far too deep for a first night. I ached to do anything but talk but this, awkward and difficult as it was, bumbly and verbally befuddled as I was, was, unfortunately, the right thing to do.

Jun stared into my eyes as if trying to divine my heart. Something inside her assented. Her answer was a kiss.

The next morning we went for a walk by the banks of the Kamo River. It was springtime and the cherry trees overhanging the river seemed to blossom in time with our footsteps. A Mexican Wave of delicate pink followed us up the river bank. Later on we went into the town. I showed Jun a shirt I was thinking about buying. On a second look it was actually pretty vile and she gently guided me towards something less migraine-inducing. Next we went to the ¥100 Shop, home of 50p bargains of all kinds. Jun picked out a plunger and, when we got home, started, unbidden, to unblock my overflowing sink. I watched in silent awe – I had never known anyone who could turn her hand to the needs of so many dimensions – plumber, fashion designer, chef, comedian, horizon-shifter, girlfriend, family member. I felt horribly flat next to her. She seemed to live in a fully three dimensional world and she was holding out an open hand to invite me into it. I felt privileged. She left later that evening telling me she had to be up early the next morning to help out her parents. She struck me as one of the most complete people I had ever met and one of the most alive. We made plans for the next weekend. It was a long week.

Chapter 20

August 19th 2004 – three years and two weeks until the crippling

Candidasa, Bali, Indonesia

I'm back in Bali this morning. Something I saw on the Breakfast News reminded me of that Balinese sunset I managed to get an accidentally great photo of. Dilapidated fishing boats silhouetted on the beach by the last rays of a sun slowly setting behind a hillside. A breakwater dissects the centre of the scene, the shoreline jutting between two stretches of shimmering sea. I have no idea quite how I managed it but it's a beautiful picture, uncluttered composition and a rare piece of pin-sharp focus.

I wish I was back there. I am in my imagination. I spend at least as much time in my memories as I do in the present. The past is much better than the present. It's that simple. Obviously I have plenty of "event" memories – wedding, Bali, Vietnam, our honeymoon – but I revel as much in the mundane – the taste of Jun's teriyaki chicken donburi[19], the smell of those Lisn Autumn Twilight incense sticks, rows of foods in the supermarket, that cheap chain izakaya[20] that keeps its beer glasses in the freezer. I wish I'd taken more photos of normal stuff. I understand conceptually that this behaviour isn't healthy but I

---

[19] 丼ぶり - bowl of rice plus a topping. Often strips of beef but Jun's speciality was teriyaki chicken.

[20] 居酒屋 – a casual restaurant/pub kind of place.

don't really know what else I can do. The difference between then and now is so huge. I can't iron my life out into a smooth continuum. It's always going to be "Before Stroke" and "After Stroke".

Part of the issue is just how easy it is to access records of past exploits. Every photo I took since 2002 is a single click away. Gmail allows me keep every last piece of mail I ever received. Flickr and Facebook have logged my every move. My current obsession is Google Street View. I ghost down the streets of my old haunts, flitting through the frozen life in the pictures. Everything is frozen. I'm not even there but I swoop in and out of the scenes. I pop into the pachinko parlour for a quick game, get my lunch from the restaurant where you order your food at a machine. You pay, it gives you a ticket then you give that to the waitress and she cooks your meal. Some days I follow the arrows as far as the "Batting Dome" in Umeda and attempt to bash the baseballs that fly out of the virtual pitcher or just hover airborne over the corrugated roof of my old house. The new tenants have taken down the elaborate aerial I had erected up there so I could get Sky TV in our inconvenient hollow.

Other days I revisit the hotels we stayed at on our honeymoon. A busy main road on Nob Hill in San Francisco and that leafy side street in New York. Everything is frozen at a specific point in time. Like me. The yellow taxi inching along 46th Street never reaches its destination and neither do I. I fly seamlessly from continent to continent, an ethereal presence among the statues. Some days I relive special moments from my life. Other days I just pop to the supermarket and get some groceries.

Today I'm back in Bali replaying scenes from our first proper holiday together. I find myself with the terrible urge to risk assess locations in my memory, to catalogue the specifics of why it would be impossible for me to enjoy these things ever again. We stayed in a chalet up a hillside. It was wonderful. A bathroom open to the stars, a veranda overlooking the pool and the novelty of affordable room service. But how would I even get there now? We were up four or five flights of rough hewn, handrail-less sets of steps up to our room. Nowadays I couldn't possibly walk up there and there were no ramps for a wheelchair. We would start the day with a dip in the pool. I can swim with a strap-on float but do they even have those kind of things in Bali? It's beside the point anyway – I could throw myself in well enough but I couldn't possibly manage the vertical stepladder to get out. We travelled most places on the back of motorbikes, paying the drivers the equivalent of a few yen a time. Who would dare to take me now? Could I even get a leg over a bike saddle anymore? What about the beach? Even if I didn't need to clamber over rocks to get down there I doubt the sandy surface would aid my shuffling gait. Soft to fall on I'll grant you but I have enough trouble walking on a solid surface let alone something that constantly shifts beneath my feet. We explored Candidasa, the little village where we stayed, on foot most of the time, took trips to the boho enclave of Ubud and spent an afternoon playing a gamelan leant to us by natives on a deserted beach we discovered down a dusty track. The walking required to do any of these things would have been impossible. One afternoon while Jun was snoozing I snuck off and bought her an afternoon session in a local spa. Massage, a reflexology session to be finished off with an "aromatic flower bath" – blossom petals floating on top of the water. She seemed to like it. I couldn't possibly sort out something like that on my own anymore. I couldn't manage the steps up to the reception for a start. No chance of getting Jun a surprise present if I need her help to get the shops. Even the photos that provide me with a breadcrumb trail back over the oceans wouldn't be possible. I gave up my swanky camera and bought an idiot-proof point-and-shoot but I still can't take a decent photo anymore. Try twiddling the settings and keeping the frame steady one handed next time you're snapping away. It's fucking hard. I rarely have anything I want to record these days but, if I do, the results are generally appalling.

All this stuff is gone now. Photos on an external hard drive loaded from old computer to new computer. But they're photos of *me*. I was fucking *there*! Fucking Bali! That was me, fucking me! Until I actually went "Bali" was pretty much shorthand for "Paradise". It was warm and tropical. Large-breasted natives garlanded themselves with strings of flowers and danced by torches in simple joy. It seemed so far away, so exotic and removed from my work-a-day existence. If I hadn't seen it with my own eyes I would have almost doubted its actual existence. It was a Xanadu, a Shangri-La, a place of dreams and magic. Then I went there. I went fucking *there.* I'm certain that I'll never go again. It wasn't as magical as I imagined but it was a real place. Now it's back to being a fantasy. But now I know that it really exists but I'll never get back there. That is unbearably worse.

Chapter 21

August 16th 2005 – 2 years and one month until the crippling

Mui Ne, Vietnam

A Mercedes people carrier picked us up from the airport. Me and Jun straggled out of the arrivals hall. I loved the visa in my passport, the red star staring at me like an accusation. I'd loved the contempt I'd been treated with while getting it in the "Vietnamese Consulate of Osaka". I'd taken an afternoon off work and got very lost looking for this place. The day had been unforgivingly hot. The sun beat mercilessly as I trudged past identical looking office blocks. I'd assumed the "Vietnamese Consulate of Osaka" would be a fairly grand building, flags fluttering and blacked out diplomatic limousines fanned around outside. Why couldn't I find a building that looked like that? Because it didn't exist. The place I eventually found was a 5th floor office in a shabby building, ancient posters of Angkor Wat peeled from the walls. The ground floor of our house was bigger. The guy at the desk had been happy enough to take my money and stick the visa in my passport but had thrust it back at me with some smirking words of Vietnamese which could have been "Enjoy your trip to my beautiful country!" or just as easily "Die a painful death, imperialist oppressor!".

There was a middle-aged man standing at the Arrivals Gate. Brown Nehru jacket and trousers, he waved a board with my name printed on it. He led us to the people carrier and loaded our luggage in. I was nerve-janglingly tired. Too many gin and tonics on the flight and not enough sleep had caught up with me. I let my head fall back onto the back of the seat. The driver closed the door, sealing our hermetic bubble from the outside world. As we inched through crowded Ho Chi Minh streets watching families of five crammed on to one moped and kids playing in unpaved streets, it began to rain. Fat, lazy tropical drops ran down the windscreen. I was glad I was inside.

We'd arrived at night and not been fit to do anything but tumble into bed but the morning bought appreciative "Matt! Wow!"'s and "Jun, look!"'s. Our room was luxurious and decorated with much more coordination than the hotchpotch we managed at home, a delightful melange of matching linen and tropical beach objets d'art. Open the front door, step on to our little balcony, trip down a couple of steps and we were on the beach. The sea was no more 50 yards away.

These holidays were amazing to me. It felt weird and a little wrong that everything was so cheap, you were *supposed* to haggle at the craft markets but it just felt mean. The initial "You're having a laugh" price you were quoted was so cheap as to feel as though paying it was an insult already so to barter it even further down felt like you were taking the piss. Battering someone down from "a chocolate bar in Osaka" to "half a chocolate bar in Osaka" seemed churlish but, then, not to barter at all seemed patronising. Uneasy ethical concerns aside this economic inequality allowed us access to things we could never consider at home. Drivers waiting at airports with our name on a board, room service just because we couldn't be bothered to walk 50 yards to the bar, rooms on the beach. I still remember Jun's simple glee at how cheap a lobster main course was. Living in the world's 6th

most expensive city meant that most anywhere was cheaper but here the differential was stark.

Me and Jun both worked hard and earned a decent amount of money but it never seemed to go quite far enough and it was hard to understand how a simple change of location suddenly made us rich. Still it didn't bother us too much as we splashed about in the waves and enjoyed daily epicurean delights. We didn't feel like we deserved all this luxury and it took us a while to understand what it enabled us to do. Taxis weren't a rainy day luxury but simply the most efficient way of getting about. We took one to the White Sand Dunes.

A guide book "must see", they were big sand dunes on the edge of a seeming desert. Sand dunes indicated to me that the sea should be peeked over the next crest but these dunes were defiantly inland. A bunch of raggedy kids appeared from nowhere with big plastic sheets for us to sled down. We climbed to the top of the hill and sat down atop the bags. Me and Jun locked eyes and smiled before we slid down the slope cackling hysterically, uncontrollably. Inevitably when we were finished, exultant and tired, the kids starting acting up. We had told one particular little guy that we would pay him to be our guide/plaggy bag porter but now all his pals started complaining. They'd all tagged along uninvited and not really provided any assistance aside from ambience creation. Now there were crocodile tears and tales of paternal beatings from other days when they had returned home empty handed. I stuck to my guns, distributed the promised dongs, grabbed Jun's hand and dragged her as quickly as I could through the clingy sand toward our waiting lift.

We stayed in the resort for dinner that night. Jun had caught the sun during the course of the day. She had the typical Japanese woman's desire for paleness but I thought she looked wonderful, alive and vibrant. Candles flickered as we ate and drank. I sat back in chair. I couldn't see the sea in the darkness but I could hear the waves gently lapping at the shore. I smiled and Jun smiled back. This was a sun-kissed instant of genuine happiness. Finite for sure but real and undeniable At times like this I was scared to tell Jun how happy I felt. It was almost too much joy for one body to contain. Pull the ring pull on my happiness, try to explain further than the general "good vibes" we were both experiencing and I would froth over like a shook up can of fizzy pop. I would gush and embarrass Jun. We didn't do "gush". I wanted to save this moment and put a little vial of it in my work bag. A quick nip on the train of a morning would let me coast through the day. I struggled to put this in perspective. I couldn't really work out how I'd got here. I was born in Coventry and grew up in Loughborough. Now I lived in Japan and holidayed in Vietnam. For the majority of the day I spoke a language other than what I had learnt growing up. I was usually timid and unadventurous, a creature of habit. I understood that these things were possible to do but I didn't understand how *I* could possibly have done them and how it all felt so natural now. Things like *this* didn't happen to people like *me*. Never mind – here I was now. I deserved this. I'd dared to break a cycle and this was my reward.

I'd been a secondary school teacher in Sheffield in 2000. I wasn't a great teacher but I was OK, getting better. I struggled to pay off student loans and couldn't afford a car. I lived in a shared house with university friends who hadn't wanted to move away. I'd had one spectacularly unsuccessful year in London before I'd run home, tail between my legs. Life was OK. I smoked too much pot and mountain biked in the Peak District at the weekends. The only problem was that I could see my life stretching out in front of me: Years would pass. I would buy a little house in a decent part of town. Maybe get married. Blag a few promotions, become a head of year. There was nothing wrong with that life and from my hospital bed it felt like a dream but then I felt like I just wanted something different for a little while before I settled into the long haul of responsible adulthood. My last adventure. My first adventure to be honest. I'd never done anything unequivocally CAPITAL LETTER and **bold "EXCITING"**. I'd done plenty of "stuff" but never anything that would surprise anybody – "Matt did a teaching qualification? Good for him – that's the kind of thing I could imagine him doing."

Japan had a lot of things going for it. It had always seemed like a pretty exciting country – the most alien place left - "Akira", "Godzilla", temples, bullet trains, tea ceremonies and schoolgirl panty vending machines. Plus it was advanced technologically and had Western standards of living. I didn't want to rough it. And there was a lot of neon. I loved neon. And, crucially, I could make a living. The teacher exchange scheme run by the Japanese government paid a decent wage. I could experience something new and pay off some debts at the same time.

I'd applied for the same scheme and been rejected when I first left university. It was primarily designed for new graduates with no teaching experience. Later, with a few years of teaching experience and a tiny bit of "man of the world" savoir faire, I passed the interview second time around. Where in Japan you ended up was random but somehow my number came up and I landed in Kyoto in July of 2000. It was everything a new visitor to Japan could hope for. Japanese people go there to see how Japan is *supposed* to be. A city of thousands of temples and shrines and religious festivals that take over the town centre seemingly most weekends. Geisha could occasionally be glimpsed scurrying down side streets. My nearest shopping arcade was half chain stores and half temples. The scent of incense mingling with the sickly smell of sweet pancakes.

I'd initially planned to stay for a year but each time I had to decide whether to renew my contract something made me stay. Maybe I wanted to do a Japanese language exam in a few months or "what was the point of going home now when I was just starting to feel settled". One year became two then three. Then I met Jun and moved to Osaka with her. The cycle of living and learning began all over again in a new city and with a new way of living. When I finally left I'd been there for nearly eight years. I'd still be there if I had my way. I'd come to Japan to escape my "real" life but had found a realer, more vivid life than I could ever have imagined. In that candle-lit restaurant in Vietnam I was surrounded by the unassailable realities of my life: smiling Jun, fancy food, luxurious room awaiting our return and palm trees wafting gently over our heads. I still struggled to understand how I'd made the decisions that had led me here. I'd never expected any of this. I'd taken myself by utter surprise.

We finished our dinner and headed out. We had to walk a few yards on the beach to get to our bungalow. Pausing for a moment, we kicked off our flip-flops and sat down, sand between our toes. I put my arm over Jun's shoulders. Neither of us said anything. We listened to the sea and filled our lungs with the tangy air. I hoped Jun felt as blissful and serene as I did. Jun leant over and kissed me as if to say "I do". Tomorrow would be just like today and that was good.

Chapter 22

May 14th 2006 - 2 years and 5 months until the crippling

Nakatsu, Osaka, Japan

Sunday morning. Me and Jun have just made love. It had been pretty spectacular. Best for a while. We'd really gone to town on each other. Sweaty and satisfied, we collapsed on either side of the bed. Now we had given up smoking the question of what to do afterwards became an issue. A gentle way to start the transition back into reality. Jun normally went downstairs and brought back a couple of glasses of juice, ice cubes in to give them a bit of status while I lit up the Autumn Twilight. We did this today but instead of rejoining me under the duvet to enjoy the last embers of the glow we had created Jun passed me a glass and went over to sit on the sofa.

The upstairs of our place was all open plan. Maybe 60 feet by 20. At one end was our double mattress and at the other end of the room was the sofa that our landlord had donated. To one side were the sliding glass doors out onto the little balcony where we kept our washing machine and dried our clothes. About two thirds of the way down the space there was a set of sliding doors so you could, if you wanted to, create a barrier between the bed and the sofa and make the space more like a "living room" and a "bedroom". We rarely did though, perhaps if we had visitors. The upshot of all this description is that, from my position in bed, I can see Jun in the "living room" bit of the space. She's sat silent on the sofa. She's not watching the TV or anything and I wonder if she's upset about something. Maybe it's something I've done. I make a mental run-through of our recent interactions and can't think of anything out of the ordinary. We had woken up at around the same time and found that our schedules synched up nicely. We'd had good sex. I'd had a great time and I'm pretty sure that Jun had too. In that moment of post-coital warmth and self-confidence I just assumed that Jun had had her world so comprehensively rocked that she needed a bit of private time to recover. The Autumn Twilight continued to edge down. I drained my apple juice and lay back on the pillow.

I woke up a little while later, could have been 2 minutes later or it could have been 2 hours. I looked at my watch – it had actually been about 15 minutes. Jun was still on the sofa. The burgundy leatherette of the sofa clashing with her orange checked boxer shorts and the star-patterned blue vest top she was wearing. I was lonely and I wanted Jun to snap out of her reverie.

"Good morning, Junkovski" I cooed from the bed, "Shall I go to Yami Yogurt in a minute? What do you want?"

Still no answer. I must have done something really bad but I had no idea what. I got out of bed and walked over to sit beside Jun. I put my arm around her shoulders. She suddenly snapped back into consciousness.

"I couldn't talk" she murmured.

"I know," I smirked, "It was pretty good, eh?"

"No! I really couldn't talk. I was sat here and everything else was fine but I couldn't get my mouth to talk. My brain wasn't working." Jun sounded scared. She was trying to explain what had happened in English but not really finding the words. It sounded disconcerting but I wasn't sure it was that different to how I sometimes felt after a good go round. I held Jun's hand and made consoling noises not thinking this was anything out particularly out of the ordinary.

But Jun was proper worried and, as it turned out, rightly so. She made a doctor's appointment. He listened to her tale and immediately referred her to a hospital. We went a few weeks later and met the white-coated doctor. This was at a proper hospital, scary and mysterious. People in wheelchairs rolled by and nurses rushed past us looking busy and efficient. The doctor talked to Jun for about 30 minutes. I came in with her but didn't really understand much of what was being said but it sounded pretty serious. Jun filled me in on the tube home – the doctor suspected she might be suffering from something called "Moyamoya Disease" but Jun was in safe hands as the guy we had just seen was the leading Japanese expert in this. People travelled from all over Japan to see him. The hospital was on the outskirts of Osaka. A bus and a tube away for us but pretty easy to get to. He wanted Jun to stay in hospital for a week or so to run some tests, do an angiogram and observe Jun at closer quarters.

She packed her holiday suitcase and I went up to the hospital with her on the appointed day. It felt awful leaving her behind and going back to just Sai. The house seemed very big all of a sudden. I spent as much time at the hospital as I could. Jun seemed in decent spirits jumping through all the hoops she need to. They had a rooftop garden for the patients and we would take our convenience store cans of coffee on to a bench out there. Jun was sharing her room with youngsters (Moyamoya is more prevalent among children) so I spent time playing Mario Kart on the DS with one of her roommates. I didn't really know what to do. Jun didn't look "sick" but this was all being taken very seriously. Jun spent all day in her slippers and dressing gown. I didn't like to see her acting so "invalid". She was strong. One day when I was visiting Jun's sister, Takako-san, happened to be there as well. She offered to treat me to tea but I declined as politely as I could. I went home and started a Tumblr blog to try to kill some time. Messing about with all the settings wasted some time but it was a pretty pointless exercise. I had nothing I particularly wanted to share with the world so in desperation I embedded the video of The Fall's "There's a Ghost in my House". That was just illogical - there was no ghost in my house. Just me and Sai and a big empty Jun-shaped space.

When Jun came home the diagnosis of Moyamoya was official. Some blood vessels in her head became constricted meaning that sometimes parts of her brain became starved of oxygen hence the inability to speak. Also increasingly she would have periods when her left arm shook uncontrollably. They suggested an operation. They would take blood vessels from her thigh and transplant them on top of her skull to compensate for the deficiencies, kind of like an internal wig. The problem was that it didn't always work. Jun was not keen to have her skull sliced open on the off-chance. I can't say I blamed her.

As she returned to her day-to-day life she seemed to me as though she had lost some of her sparkle. Unsurprising really when you were being urged to think seriously about brain surgery. She didn't seem to laugh anymore. She began to go to bed even earlier in the week – pretty much – home, tea, bath, bed. I was accustomed to her early nights but suddenly felt alone, adrift. Her weekends would be spent sleeping. I got used to spending Saturday's browsing second hand record shops on my own. Whatever I tried, whatever trinkets I bought for her, whatever DVD's I rented ("Groundhog Day" isn't called that in Japanese and I spent mortifying moments at the video shop counter trying to explain the plot of the film in pidgin Japanese and asking if they had it) I couldn't reach her and I slowly became frustrated. I wasn't as supportive as I should have been. I just wanted everything to go back to how it was before. I just wanted my old Jun back and thought I could cajole and pester it into reappearing. Obviously, with hindsight, I can understand a little of how an illness can affect you psychologically and perhaps a tiny bit about how a potential medical catastrophe hanging over your head can make you feel but back then I wasn't so aware. This is no excuse. A lack of understanding or empathy in no way justifies my behaviour. I failed as a human being. Since I eventually grew up a little there haven't been too many things that I've done that I'm actively ashamed of but this would be one of them. Whether I understood or not, whether Jun wanted to talk or not, I had a duty to support her and give her the space to get her head around being sick. Instead I behaved pretty disgracefully – telling her she ought to be more considerate as a person to be around in spite of everything, that I deserved a bit more respect. Trying to chivvy her along. Maybe some fried chicken from Family Mart would make her feel better? The latest Saw film? A weekend at an onsen? Nothing I bought for her seemed to help. Jun didn't want to talk about it and I kept trying to drag something out. I should have given her more space and time just to be. Sitting her on the bed one sunny Saturday morning and pretty much telling her to "pull herself together". I now know from bitter experience that this kind of thing is exactly what is not required.

Interrogation and instruction is no use to anyone. I acted exactly the way that I hate people to act around me now. Telling her how she ought to feel. I was scared. Jun was having a terrifying time and I couldn't help. She didn't want to talk about it with me. I felt powerless. Fear made me act like a pig. There's no excuse.

As the months passed Jun became worried about taking the train by herself. I never really got it verbalised by her but I think it must have been that she was scared that something would happen to her while she was by herself in the carriage. She must have been worried in case anything worse than what had already been happening to her happened while she was alone. It made her hour-each-way commute an every day torture. Panic would often shoo her off the train and she would have to walk alongside the tracks for the last few stops. She told me about this sometimes but I suspected there were a lot of times that she kept it to herself. A few times I would come and meet her halfway on the way back from work of an evening. I'd be stood there at Nishinomiyakitaguchi station scanning the concourse for Jun, not really understanding what I was doing but glad to be able to do *something* all the same. Day-to-day I felt excluded from what was going on in Jun's head. I wanted to help but didn't seem able to grasp the shape of things. I blundered about trying to find solutions to a problem I couldn't really understand. Jun didn't want to talk about it and I didn't know how to broach it in a way that encouraged Jun to try. I did all the things I now know are not helpful to someone struggling with ill health. Giving advice rather than trying to listen. Too much "should" and not enough "could". Looking for one-stop explanations and resolutions rather than just accepting the amorphous nature of how things were. I still thought that every problem had to have a solution Whenever I tried to talk about it came out as though I was telling Jun off. Sometimes I think maybe I was.

Chapter 23

October 7th 2006 - 11 months until the crippling

Osaka, Japan

I proposed to Jun in bed one Saturday morning. I'd arranged for us to go on a surprise trip to Barcelona at Christmas and I'd been planning to do it then but had chickened out for reasons I didn't quite understand. I was sure that I wanted to do it and I was sure that Jun would say yes. I had some reservations about marriage – I didn't need a ring to prove my love. Japanese wedding ceremonies are often ludicrous affairs of numerous costume changes, laser illuminated karaoke and elaborate headgear. I didn't want any of this and I didn't think Jun did either but even the simplest wedding ceremony seemed like a lot of unnecessary hassle. I was pretty sure I would shrivel and die if I left Jun and I was quietly confident that she kind of liked me so where was the need?

So why had I proposed then? I think I had come to understand that Jun was just better than I could possibly ever deserve. I was clearly punching way above my weight and I didn't want it to be too easy for her to escape when she did finally come to her senses. She was kind and organised, practical and understanding, sexy and funny. We'd been living together in (almost) perfect harmony for over three years. We never really talked about it but I got a sense that she would like it. Co-habitation isn't quite so common in Japan as it is in the West. Co-habiting with a foreigner rarer still. A marriage would make things as legitimate in the eyes of the world as they seemed to us. Plus being officially married would make Jun's visa that much easier to acquire when we eventually came to England . I was self-righteously confident that, as a British Citizen, I would have no problem getting my life-partner back into the country with me but Jun was terrified of customs and visa stuff. She had a ready supply of stories of denied visas and refused entries. As scarily symbolic of "being a grown up" as marriage was I had slowly realised that I was living a "grown-up" life whatever my marital status was. Restaurants and short breaks away dominated our weekends not clubs and binge drinking. We chose curtains together and shared the cooking. We knew each other's parents. We were living the life so we may as well have the day and get the presents.

So I nervously proposed in stumbling Japanese. This being the one sentence I couldn't get Jun to correct in advance for me. Thankfully she accepted although I did seem to catch a faint whiff of "finally!" in the air. I hadn't got her an engagement ring. I should have. We decided on an autumn wedding. That gave us more than enough time to get everything sorted out. Apart from going up to ask Adachi-san formally for his daughter's hand in marriage nothing really changed for a few weeks.

Then, slowly at first but with an inexorably increasing pace, we had to do *stuff*. We were both set on not having a super-expensive wedding but didn't want something cheap and nasty. We were, thankfully, in agreement, about what kind of thing we wanted but it seemed impossible to find a venue that could cater for us. Everywhere was either too gaudy and marbled or too paper peeling and sticky floored. That was whole weekends taken up. You'd visit a potential place, realise it was no good as soon as you entered the building and then have to listen to two hours of spiel and take a guided tour of the venue from an enthusiastic member of staff before you could escape. Japanese weddings had to have two venues. Somewhere for the ceremony and then somewhere for an evening meal. Everything in the same place – heaven forbid! We were only planning on having 30 or so people there. I, especially, didn't know too many people to invite. I had some friends coming over for it from England which made me feel very privileged. They happen to be vegetarians. Japanese catering often doesn't get the concept of "vegetarianism" so that was another challenge.

We finally settled on a place that was just about in our budgetary range. It purported to be the "cheapest wedding venue in Osaka" and it perhaps was if you got married in your jeans in silence, drank nothing but water and were in and out of the building within 10 minutes. By the time we had added in all "optional extras" like music, photos, food and flowers the "cheapest wedding in Osaka" was proving surprisingly expensive. The place had the added advantage of providing a one-stop shopping experience. We could borrow costumes, eat our lunch, print the invitations, organise the flowers and get the photo albums made up all under one roof. That should simplify things a bit, eh?

Not. A. Bit. Of. It.

Even with so much stuff taken care of for us there was still a seemingly endless stream of more *stuff*. I was sent to print out the invitations. We were trying to save money by doing it ourselves. The poor Kinko's staff had as little idea of what was going on as I did. I think I went three times before I got it right. I had to location scout hotels for my English guests and we had to decide on the presents to give to guests as they left. Ceremonial gift giving is a big deal and Jun wanted to get it right. The custom was that guests gave you an envelope of cash on arrival (already earmarked to pay for the venue and all the services) and then they would get a bag of presents when they left. This is important, has to be done properly and has to have a decent cash value. With a lot of this stuff I just put my hands up, decided this was nuanced Japanese stuff that I would never understand and simply devolved myself from any part of the decision making process. Jun had to carry a disproportionate amount of weight. I remember one day coming home from work and Jun started bombarding me with questions before I had even got my shoes off and got in the house. I was pissed off and angry at the time but perhaps if I had taken a more active role in helping to plan and organise the day then things would have been different?

One part of the preparations that I was unequivocally enthusiastic about was choosing my clothes. Jun had got a dress made during a recent trip to Thailand but she didn't like it to much in the cold light of our bedroom mirror so she opted to borrow some dresses from the venue. She found a lovely wedding dress and then a pretty orange confection for lunch. I dutifully rooted through the hangers but I found nothing that fitted in with my self image – too lilac or too peppermint or too ruffly or too coat-taily or too top-hatty. There was nothing for it – I was going to have to buy a suit. I liked clothes but I had very little interest in male tailoring. All the same I approached this process with a genuine desire to educate myself in the ways of the cloth. One breast or two? How many sleeve cuff buttons? Double or single vent? Turnups? Pleats? What was the best way to disguise my fledgling beer gut? I decided that bespoke tailoring was the only way forward. It wasn't *hideously* expensive and, hey, I was only going to do this once. This was forever. Besides I was feeling a little dislocated from the whole "wedding" project and this was a good chance to build a little "Matt" back into the process. And the tailor was next to our favourite bagel shop. "While we're here we might as well..."

Every adult male in Japan has a black suit for formal occasions. Not just for funerals. A black suit is the correct item of clothing for a wedding, be it your's or someone else's. As such once I'd told the tape measure-wielding member of staff that this suit was for my wedding it took every inch of Japanese I had to explain that I didn't actually want a black suit for myself. I eventually ended up with a mid-grey, single-breasted, single vented, pleat-less number. I looked Don Draper-smart, just the correct amount of shirt cuff protruding. The best thing was my name embroidered on the inside just below the pocket. Not a first-day-of-term sewn in name tag but a proper textured, raised, joined-up piece of embroidery. I should have got them to embroider something witty or romantic instead of my name – the date of the wedding or Jun's name or "Bad Motherfucker" or something – but I wasn't quick thinking enough. A simple white shirt, a Paul Smith paisley tie and a nice pair of Clarks slip-ons and I was ready. Even if I do say so myself, I looked *ace*.

The weeks before the wedding rushed by. Last minute dashes to the venue, keeping my English guests amused, writing speeches, getting rings engraved and generally panicking. In all this hubbub we almost forgot that we actually got married in the midst of it all. The extravaganza that we were ineptly attempting to orchestrate was no more than a formality. It had no legal meaning whatsoever. The formal ceremony was nothing more than a symbol. It was a chance for us to emerge into society as a married couple. The actual wedding ceremony was nothing more than a trip to the local council offices with the appropriate I.D. and do a bit of paperwork. It took no more than half an hour and was perhaps the simplest part of the whole experience. It was also my favourite part – the steamy cocoon in the back of the taxi as we travelled there in the autumn fog, the feeling of a secret that only me and Jun shared for a few days. We spent a conspiratorial weekend together before we divulged the news to anyone else. This was something that was only shared between us, an anonymous council bureaucrat and the taxi driver. For once the uniform that every taxi driver wore, the white gloves and the peaked admiral's cap, seemed perfectly appropriate.

When the day of the wedding came round we were both a bit sick of the whole process, nervous and desperate to get the bloody thing done. In the taxi up to chapel we debated sacking off the whole shebang, and just moving straight on to the honeymoon. Diverting the taxi to the airport would be no problem but unfortunately our flights were not for another three months. When we got there Jun was whisked off to be dressed and, once I had convinced incredulous staff members that I would be staying in the suit I had come in, I had nothing to do but hang about corridors drinking gallons of canned coffee and trying not to get in the way of the couples booked in before us or intrude in their photographs.

We had chosen to have the ceremony in the rooftop garden area but the inevitable rain drove us into an indoor chapel. Jun's Dad led her down the aisle. She looked amazing. I felt blessed. The ceremony began. The guy running the ceremony said some stuff I didn't understand. Jun said some stuff I had had her translate for me in our living room a few days ago. When it came to me I parroted the Japanese vows I had memorised phonetically. I was glad when the talking bits were done and the guy told me and Jun that we could kiss. Finally a bit I could understand. We left the chapel to "Baby I love you" by The Ramones. We had lunch and speeches at the chapel. Soon the guests were getting ready to move on to the next venue and we were in the back room fishing their cash out of ornate envelopes and handing it over to the chapel manager. They expected to be paid on the day. Never have I received and lost so much money so quickly. Still other people's generosity picked up the tab for our great day and even left us a little left over for taxis.

We had another do with some different guests in the evening. I was well behaved but by the time we arrived at the third and final stop, a cosy little bar walking distance from home, we had lost all the people we needed to behave for and me and Jun could enjoy some proper drinks and let ourselves go a bit. A woozy contentment, an exhausted sense of achievement and free sake soon washed over me and I was drunk and tired. Jun dragged me home about 1am. As we staggered home arm in arm impressionistic scenes from the day swam through my mind – arriving a little too early for the evening meal we had gone to a cafe across the road for a coffee, Jun had looked so beautiful and, eyes meeting over the cups, we managed to share a moment of quiet private joy during a very public day, how great it was for my football mate, Miyan, to suddenly appear part-way through the evening, how well my friends from different continents who had no way of communicating aside from body language seemed to get on, how great our friends Hiromi and Eriko and Euan had been at doing all those wedding day necessities, making speeches or corralling guests from point to point. The welcome board Eriko made for us to put up outside the chapel found a home on the wall over our bed until I left Japan.

We tumbled into the house and woke up Sai. We gave him a gushing hug. Jun had already started the paperwork to officially become Junko Padmore or at least Padomoa[21] which was as close as you can get in Japanese. Maybe Sai could become Psycho Padmore? How would we do that? Our butterfly minds flitted onto the next thing. Nomenclature issues would have to wait for another day. The stairs beckoned. We staggered up and got undressed. An expensive dress and a bespoke suit were left scattered on the tatami. We weren't seized by passion but by bone-tiredness. I managed to envelope Jun in a multi-faceted hug. If hugs could talk it would have said "Thank you for letting me part of you for ever" and "Thank you for organising nearly all of today" and "You looked so beautiful today" and "Thank you for everything that we've shared together already and that we will share in the future" and "I love you" and "I thought I wasn't bothered but actually I'm so proud that you would want to take my name". We separated. There was one last thing to do. I lit the Autumn Twilight incense stick and put my head on the pillow. I was asleep almost straightaway. Tiny fingers of fragrant smoke embraced us as we slept.

[21] パドモア - "Padomoa" is as close as you can get to my surname in the Japanese pronunciation system.

Chapter 24

21st December 2006 - 10 months until the crippling

San Francisco and New York, United States of America

Our honeymoon planning kept us going through the wedding planning. As it got closer to the day it felt more and more as though the least important factors in the whole wedding situation were us, the bride and groom. Our thoughts seemed more and more geared towards getting things right for our guests. The honeymoon, however, was just about us. Deciding, booking and organising something exclusively for ourselves provided a welcome break and I had no excuse not to engage. We loved holidays and this was a perfect chance to do something a bit special.

Our first plan was Costa Rica. We fancied greenery and volcanoes, lodges and trekking. Unfortunately the Japanese travel industry has an intricate and frustrating logic of its own. Nowhere could sell us flights to Costa Rica, the tickets hadn't been released yet. What they *could* tell us was that tickets on the same flights were already on sale in North America and were almost sold out. They would probably be gone by the time we got a crack at them but it was not a problem as first class tickets would most likely still be available. No issue for the travel agent's commission but an insurmountable problem for our finances. Surely there was a way that people could get two people between Costa Rica and Japan for less than the price of a small car? There probably was but we couldn't work it out. Giving up on that idea we thought about Iceland until some idle googling revealed that it was only going to be light for 4 hours a day when we would be there. We wanted to relax and take it easy but maybe not quite *that* easy. Stymied again we rethought. Racking our brains for ideas we switched the telly on and there it was – a cheaply shot documentary about an Amtrak train trip across America. I'd always fancied doing something like that and, after a bit of convincing, Jun agreed. It was perfect – Jun fancied herself as a bit of a backpacker and liked to rough it out of a rucksack while I was a bit more genteel. I liked hotels and a bit of luxury. It was the best of both worlds – nice hotels at either end of the train journey in San Francisco and New York and a bit of acceptably unrough roughing it on the 3-day train in-between. Plus it was cheap. Amtrak is not a leisure choice for most Americans so it was priced like a train trip rather than a holiday.

I'd been upgraded on my flight home once before but had been too hung-over to appreciate it. When you're desperately trying keep your lunch down leg room is not a huge issue. This time would be different. We called Korean Air pretending to be a well-wishing wedding guest and informed them that Mr and Mrs Padmore would be catching a flight as part of their honeymoon –

"Could you do maybe do something to make the flight special?"

"Of course, Mr Smith, leave it to us. Thanks for letting us know."

I put the phone down with a smirk of satisfaction and leant over to kiss Jun. That was that sorted. They'd be bound to upgrade us now. It was an unwritten law that honeymooners got the good stuff. I lay back on the sofa and daydreamed of endless high end liquor and leather upholstery.

We got a cake. A not-very-nice, hard to juggle through an airport, kid's birthday party size cake. We'd snogged at the check-in and made puppy dog faces as the suitcases conveyor-belted away.

"Mr and Mrs Padmore – we know it's a special trip for you so we have something extra-special for you to help you remember it by."

The lady behind the check-in desk reached down and began to extract a box from a bag. We watched with bated breath. What could it be? Stickers proclaiming us to be honeymooners and therefore to be extended every possible courtesy? Vouchers to spend in Duty-Free? With a flourish the lady opened up the box to reveal a garish cake – too many chocolate shavings, an artery-clogging amount of cream and a plastic tree's worth of glace cherries. With a crestfallen "thanks" we took the cake and headed for the plane. We tried to be pleased. We tried to eat it but it was just sickly mess, tasting of frosting and dashed expectations. If it had been a wedding dress it would have been flouncy, many layered and topped off with too much pink lace. Its final destination was a rubbish bin in Seoul during our stopover. The hassle of dragging it through post 9/11 customs and pretending to each other that we liked the taste too much for even our "first day of honeymoon" elation. Even if it had been worth saving, the chances of it making it to America in any kind of edible form were about nil. We'd saved it a life of pain and humiliation.

Our first stop was San Francisco. We left no tourist cliché unturned. We clung onto the side of trams and acted tough in Alcatraz. We walked down the famous zigzag street and bought tourist tat at Fisherman's Wharf. As hackneyed as all this might have been it seemed like it had all been laid on especially for us. The sea lions at the harbour had swum in from the Pacific Ocean just for us and the cantankerous Chinese lady selling tram tickets was an extra employed purely to provide colour and anecdote to our reminiscences. Audio tours and guidebooks were put together with us in mind. The single malt in the hotel bar had been distilled ten tears previously to the exact tastes of my palate. The Thai restaurant just down the hill from the hotel knew how to make green curry just the way Jun liked it.

We boarded the train on Christmas Morning. It was a trip scheduled for 72 hours but it ended up taking a day longer than that. It was magnificent. Parts of America are still stupendously beautiful. There were landscapes of stern looking mountain ranges, dramatic rock formations, tumbleweed plains, tunnels wending for miles at a time and pine trees as far as the eye could see. Conductors pointed out interesting features on the Tannoy as we rolled by: That was "the most expensive stretch of highway in the world" and that mine had been "robbed by Butch Cassidy and the Sundance Kid". Meals were included. You went to the Dining Car and shared your table with other travellers. This was a great way to meet real-life Americans and the resulting encounters gave us no end incredulous giggles and "did you hear what he said?!"'s back in the safety of our cabin. The cabin was brilliant, a triumph of ingenuity and compact design. The toilet was under Jun's seat. One of had to leave the room if the other person wanted to use it. We were intimate but not *that* intimate. (In less than a year Jun and me would be in a hospital toilet together. She would be frantically trying to wipe shit off my arse and pants while I swayed on a grab rail unused to standing without a physio present.) I slept above the window in what looked like a luggage rack. The netting held me in, our luggage was stashed elsewhere.

Snow over the mountains was slowing us down. One night as we slept and the train chugged over The Rockies we stopped. There were often brief delays as the driver waited for signals to change or points to adjust but this hold-up was for much longer. The lack of a reassuring rocking in our bunks woke both me and Jun up. I rolled out of the top bunk and joined Jun below. We both peered out of the cabin window. The sight that greeted us was breathtaking. There, 100 million miles above us, were stars. They glinted and twinkled with a brightness and a pin-prick luminosity I had never seen before or seen since. The North Star, The Plough, Ursa Major and other half-remembered stars from primary school. I couldn't recognise any of these things but I could suddenly see clearly how people could have done. The stars were stitches in the sky above Colorado making shapes and patterns. It was as though we had both put much needed glasses on. Constellations suddenly sprung into proper focus. In Osaka or London or Sheffield stars were an indistinct blob. Here,high in the mountains and out of reach of light and air pollution, individual stars gained clarity and definition. Glittering above the snowy mountain tops and the pine tree silhouettes it was the most beautiful thing I have ever seen.

The snow was delaying us pretty badly. The rumour in the Buffet Car was that if you had a connection to make in Chicago you would probably miss it. We were due to catch the train to New York from there and it didn't sound like we would make it. Travellers desperate to cross the country to spend the festive period with loved ones were understandably fed up but we weren't particularly bothered. We were on an adventure and adventure could be found anywhere. The conductor assured us that we would be put up in a hotel in Chicago while we awaited the next once-a-day train. The train eventually dragged itself into Chicago half a day late. Our connection was long since missed but Amtrak organised things as well as the conductor said they would. We were put up in a swanky hotel much nicer than we could ever afford ourselves. The bed in our room had thirteen pillows on it. The vast majority of them ended up tossed on the floor but I was impressed enough by the very idea of such a thing that I counted them and recorded the number in my notebook next to Jun's cartoon drawing of the Chicago Bulls logo. Amtrak sorted us out with spending money and cab fare and we ended up with a day off the guidebook grid. We did little aside from wander around the centre of the city but a bit of freestyling was appreciated by us both.

When we eventually got back on the train for the final stretch to New York it was like reuniting with an old friend and we were sad to get off at the bustle of Penn Station. We eased slightly off the tourist trail over the next few days but still found time for Central Park and some art galleries. We had dinner one night in a proper diner, ungentrified with peeling upholstery on the seats in our booth. In the booth opposite us were five cops. Their guns sat menacingly on their hips and their walkie-talkies squawked constantly as they munched their fries and bitched about overtime.

We spent New Year's Eve in our hotel room. We'd tried to get into Times Square but had been turned away by cops trying to control revellers. I think we were in bed by before midnight. Never mind - we'd do something wild next year. We left on the 2nd of January and were back in Japan to dish out omiyage at belated Oshougatsu[22] celebrations as we fought our jetlag. We shared our photos around but the trip felt like our secret.

---

[22] お正月 – Japanese New Year Festival. The most important festival in the year. As big a deal as Christmas in the West .

Chapter 25

August 18 2007 – three weeks to the crippling

Ishigaki Island, Okinawa, Japan

I'm staring at the photo on my screen. We're on a shingly riverbank on an overcast day. I'm in shorts and a black over-the-head cagoule. Jun is in black leggings and a turquoise t-shirt, hair tied back as it usually was. Our awkwardly worn life jackets and the background canoes testify to our recent endeavours. A guide had offered to take our photo at the end of the trip. I remember standing there, damp and tired, but glad to get a picture of me and Jun together. We didn't have many of them, we did most stuff on our own and were shy of asking randoms to snap us together. We're side by side, arms round each other. My arm appears out the other side of Jun's body but hers doesn't reach, hidden somewhere behind the small of my back.

We'd spent the afternoon canoeing lazily through a mangrove swamp. There was nothing extreme about this in anyway – we'd been picked up from and would be dropped off back at our B&B on the other side of the island. We were in a group of, maybe, 10, intrepid retirees and timid young couples. The water was so shallow we could probably have paddled just as quickly. A young couple in a two-person kayak bought their Chihuahua along complete in its own doggie life jacket. Still it was an authentic enough experience, authentic enough for us anyway. The water was cold and wet, the mud was sticky and, when we stopped in the heart of the swamp for a gooey walk the tiny crabs caressed your toes. Universal Studios Osaka this wasn't.

Looking at the photo now the weird thing to me is that my left arm is doing nothing. It hangs limply down by my side, as does Jun's. It looks pretty much like it does now but then I had a choice. I could be doing something, anything, with it. Pointing at the camera, flashing the ubiquitous Japanese peace sign, making a "comedy" salute or triumphantly waving a paddle? I lose the use of that arm forever in a little over three weeks. That photo is dated the 18th of August 2007. About three weeks later on the morning of the 6th of September, I had my stroke. That was a Thursday. We canoed on a Sunday. Why aren't I making more of an effort to use that arm I would lose so soon?

In fact, what am I doing on a small tourist island off the tip of Japan? I should be racing through the streets of Osaka and rushing into the nearest hospital and demanding to be checked out. Either that or jumping the next plane to England and staggering into the nearest hospital to the airport.

"I'm going to have a stroke in three weeks!" -Who would believe me anyway? Even if I could have explained it in my broken Japanese who is going to believe me? "I demand blood thinning drugs right now!" Running frantically, hysterically through the streets, howling my impending agony. "Soylent Green is people!" What would you think? What would I think?

I don't know what I would have done differently if I knew what was going to happen to me. Hug Jun more? It's not as though me and Jenny Agutter could have embarked on a nail-biting stroke prevention mission, a race against time.

This is part of my problem – my life story doesn't fit into a nice pattern. My arc has is just a line that suddenly stops dead. There's no satisfying three act progression. It's not a curve of full of possibilities and directions. It's a dive, a dead-end. I have a back-story but nothing out front.

If I had my time again I would probably still go canoeing up a river on Ishikgaki Island. I would be sure to get a two person kayak though.

My eye is drawn to another photo from that last holiday. A typhoon has kept us trapped in our room. We've rushed to Lawson's and stocked up on beer and snacks, excited to be part of a genuine crisis, and spent the evening watching daft Japanese telly and peering disappointedly out of the window every five minutes. No sign of a typhoon up this back road – typical Japanese over-reaction. We've gone to bed and woken up to find the invisible typhoon is still apparently tormenting the island.

I would like to go out but Jun doesn't want me to put the owners of our B&B in an awkward position so I have to stay in. The owners wouldn't want to tell me to stay in but would fret uncontrollably until I emerged intact from the imagined maelstrom.

I can't leave the room so there seems little point in getting out of bed. Our room has two single beds rather than a double and I've been mardily moaning to Jun about this since we arrived. I'm naked in bed, pale flesh protruding out of either end of the duvet. I've got a grump on – bored, awake and lonely in my single bed. I'm almost kicking the mattress in frustration. I want proper food as much as I usually love all the convenience store junk piled up in the mini fridge and the cupboards. I'm being inconvenienced by a natural disaster but denied the fun of seeing it. Jun often just leaves me be when I have a cob on but this time she's determined to snap me out of it.

She starts taking photos of my grimaces. SNAP! She clicks on my angry face and then shows me the photo of myself on the screen on the back. I look ridiculous – a toddler denied his ice-cream. She takes another and shows me. I look just as daft. Soon I'm ashamed of my immaturity and I'm gurning for the camera trying to overcompensate by being silly.

Soon I calm down and grin normally. "Cheer up Matt" mission accomplished Jun deletes the photos from the memory, smiles at my "endearing" stupidity and sets herself for a sensible picture. That's the one that I'm looking at today –

Bed not quite big enough for my 6" frame? Single occupant? White sheets? Anonymous furnishings? Unwashed, messy hair? It reminds me of nothing more than the hospital bed I know now that I would soon be in.

Part 5

Chapter 26

March 5th 2008 – 8 months since the crippling

Nakatsu, Osaka, Japan

Jun leaves for work around 6am. She rolls her futon up and puts it in the corner. I'm awake on the fold-up bed at the back of the room. She gives me a quick kiss, tells me she loves me and reminds me that there are convenience store snacks on top of the fridge for me. I spy a packet of Oreos and a chicken sandwich. The front door slides shut and she's gone. I drift back into an aimless doze.

An indeterminate amount of time later I crash-land back into reality. Looking at the clock it's about 9am. In the week I have nothing to get up for, no one to check up on me but I try to get up at a reasonable hour for some reason. It makes the days unnecessarily long, I'm immensely tired *all the time* and I feel as weak as a kitten but getting up somehow feels like something I ought to do. I swing myself out of bed and reach for the boot. I have no control over my left ankle and it droops down when I try to walk. This means I'm continually in danger of catching my foot on the floor. The hospital's solution is the "boot" – bespoke tailored at considerable cost to my exact leg size. Its off-white, semi-rigid plastic shaped like a Wellington boot with an open front. Adjustable straps across my foot, mid and upper shin keep it tight on my leg. The idea is that I wear it over my leg and foot and it keeps my ankle solid and stops it drooping down. I'm terrified to try to walk anywhere without it on. I strap it in for the 4 yard trip between the bath and my bed and if I need to go to the toilet in the middle of the night. It's an ugly, unwieldy thing and I don't understand why something that is only supposed to support my ankle needs to go all the way up to my knee. Still I dutifully strap it on, feed Sai and set the coffee machine going. Coffee filtered and a cup steaming in front of me I text Jun to say hi and wish her a bearable day at work. Next I wash my hair, careful to keep the boot dry, and get dressed.

It's 9.27am and I'm sat on the edge of the bed in pull on Patagonia pants and a hoodie. Trousers are a problem nowadays. Trying to do up a button fly on a reasonably snug pair of jeans is an impossibility. I'm lucky that I have a pair of grey paper-thin elasticated-waistband trousers that I used to wear to work in the summer. The pockets have worn through and if I forget and put change in them it falls straight to the floor down by my feet but I can get them on and I'm grateful for small mercies. I use my right hand to lift and twist my left hand into my eye line. The Paul Smith watch on my wrist now reads 9.28am. The question presents itself, as it does every morning – what on earth am I going to do today? Jun won't be back until 7 so how on earth am I going to kill the time until then?

I left the hospital on the 18th of February. Being back home was revelatory, a cavalcade of overwhelming sights and sensations. Look! Psycho! See! Internet access! Sleeping with Jun! Proper food! Jun had already booked our flights back to the UK but they were not for a month and a bit. The weekends were great. We went to restaurants, rented DVDs to watch on the tiny laptop screen and went to department stores but weekdays were a different matter entirely. While Jun was at work I had nothing to do. It was me and Sai and the internet in a strange shadowy, internal world. I knew there had to be more to life than this but I had no idea what it was and, anyway, I couldn't start it until I was back in Britain. Large parts of my life had been on hold for the 6 months that I was in hospital and now I was in a different holding pattern. I compartmentalised the day time hours into blocks – listening to that radio show on the internet took up two hours, a snooze took up an hour, half an hour for crying. I could perhaps manage to read a book for half an hour, gleaning every piece of possible information from The Guardian maybe took an hour, updating my blog took an hour. Anything to break the day into manageable chunks until Jun got back.

I had set myself challenges – that was the kind of thing that disabled people were supposed to do, right? Set yourself seemingly unattainable targets and achieve them through sheer force of will. Repeat the process enough times and you would get better. The dark days simply a memory or an inspiring anecdote for other people. My first challenge was our stairs. I'd had one quickly aborted go on the stairs in the rehab room at the hospital. For some reason they didn't allow me to use the handrail. I was supposed to just use my stick for support and not hold on to anything. This didn't work very well at all and the experiment was soon abandoned. They'd very specifically told me at the hospital that I wouldn't be able to go up the stairs in my house. My bed was upstairs so I was told that Jun had to get something for downstairs. I wasn't adept enough at getting upright so they didn't want me sleeping on a futon on the floor. We needed a bed for a month that would fit in quite a poky room. Jun ended up getting me a cheap fold up bed, pretty much an economy version of the hospital bed I had just vacated. It was not too comfortable but it was raised a foot off the floor and that made all the difference to getting up and down. I think we gave it to our next door neighbour when we left. It was a single bed. Jun slept on a futon on the floor next to me. She was good. She stayed downstairs almost as much as me. It was strange to have half of your house tantalisingly close but off-limits.

So everyday I practised. I positioned myself in front of the stairs like a horse addressing a jump and dared myself on. The flight loomed above me, my own pathetic Everest. Upstairs was a TV and a double bed. I could sleep with in the same bed as Jun. That would make this shady half-life seem slightly more real. It seemed like another world up there but I knew the geography and topography intimately. I had probably spent a year of my life up there. I could tell you exactly where the holes in the sofa were and map the contours of the artex on the walls. There was a rail on the right hand side of the stairs and luckily that matched up with my working hand. I could hold on and go up forwards. I would have to reverse down backwards as I had no way of holding on with my left hand. I stared at the stairs and they seemed to multiply and fold over themselves at impossible M.C.Escher angles. I was working on doing one extra step a day. Today was six steps. I went up without too much incident, ashamed at how scared I was, and started to back down. As nerve wracking as this was it was actually pretty easy. Still I religiously stuck to my "one step-a-day" mantra. That month would have been so much more bearable if I had managed to ascend.

That was my first challenge. The second I had set for myself was walking places. Most days I went to a nearby park for my lunch. It couldn't have been more than a hundred yards away and it wasn't very exciting but getting there and then just *being* felt like something vital and worthwhile. Me and my stick would hobble over there. Walking was still pretty scary to me. With the boot over my left foot shoes were a problem. My left foot was bulbous and over-sized. The boot was supposed to fit into your shoes but we couldn't manage it. In the end I hit on a potential solution. We headed off to Tennoji and the Birkenstock store there. I bought two pairs of identical sandals one size apart from each other. The size 10 went onto my right foot like normal and, to my relief, a size 11 could be shoehorned onto my booted left foot. The sandal gaps allowed for awkward plastic bulges to spill over the edges. Early March wasn't warm enough for bare feet so I ended up doing the sandals/socks thing that is so reviled. I actually quite liked it as a maybe fashionable piece of anti-fashion. I used to like going to the park. It was bracingly cold, there were benches to sit on and it was good to be in the open air. I optimistically took my MP3 player one day but untangling earphone cable one handed is a Sisyphean task.

I loved that park, sent Jun mobile phone photos of it but I knew I couldn't stay in it forever. I had to try further afield. My first mission was to Family Mart on the corner. This was only a little way further and had the added bonus of allowing me to reward myself with beer afterwards. Next was the Thai restaurant. That was further – under the rail bridge and around the corner. The bridge was hard to get under because the walkway roof was too low and I had to walk stooped for 20 yards. I managed it but the movement was unfamiliar enough to be disconcerting. After that I was stuck where to go. Everywhere in Nakatsu suddenly seemed a long way further and nothing seemed to present itself in convenient stages with handy benches scattered along the route. Still no one said that stopping being disabled by a force of will was going to be easy so I settled on a route in my head – under the tunnel, past the Tube station, in front of the bank, by Yami Yoghurt and close to that izakaya we liked. Ambition perhaps got the better of common sense but my heart swelled at the thought of surprising Jun with breakfast fetched from Yami Yoghurt or suggesting that we went to that izakaya for dinner. She would look so proud of me but I would say nothing and just bask.

Birks squeezed on, corduroy flat cap pulled down determinedly and scarf pulled up tight against the elements I set off. The first bit was ok. I wobbled a little on the stick and my left knee locked back judderingly with every step but I was covering the ground. Safely under the bridge and onto the main road. Cars roared by. What if I fell into the road? The pavement was busy with shoppers and parked bicycles littered my path. People stared. People stared at a gaijin normally but a gaijin who couldn't really walk properly? That was a rarity. I was getting tired, my strides getting shorter. My head started to spin. Walking still required concentration – thinking about the weight distribution between feet and stick, making sure to move everything in the right order. It went "stick and left foot forward together then right foot catches up". Get this wrong and I could end up in a right mess, poledancing uncontrollably around my stick as I slammed onto the pavement. Which is precisely what I did.

By the time I realise what's happened I'm blinking on my back on the pavement. There is a crowd of onlookers in a circle around me. I can see their shadows but the pale sun is in my eyes and I can't focus. Somebody grabs me under the shoulder and helps me up.

"Are you ok? Do you need some help?"

"I'm fine, please don't worry."

"Are you sure?"

I'm not sure. I want someone to take me home and tuck me in but even more than that I want to be alone with my shame. I want to be in a darkened room holding my humiliation close. I brusquely thank everyone for their help and point my burning cheeks towards the next stage of my journey. I'm so far from home. There would be no point turning back. It would be no quicker to get back so I carry on. I pass the bank and Yami Yoghurt but they're pyrrhic victories. The boot is rubbing on the back of my calf and hurting, a portent of a week of red raw torment. My knee aches. I'm so tired. I can barely see. Every pigeon step is a torment. I ooze sweat into my coat. I have to stop every few metres to lean on walls or perch awkwardly on protruding bits of buildings. I'm in self-inflicted agony but there's no get out. To make it end I have to prolong it. No "I'm a cripple get me out of here!"

My steps shorten and shorten. Initially I measure my stride in metres, then feet, then inches and finally centimetres. When I do finally make it home exhaustion overtakes humiliation and I tumble onto the bed and sleep. I'm woken by Jun's key in the lock. After tea I tell Jun about what happened to me making it sound like a joke, like it happened to someone else. For the rest of the time here I stick to the park on my doorstep.

Chapter 27

March 16th 2008 – 7 months and 2 weeks since the crippling

Umeda, Osaka, Japan

I'll never fucking get down there! No fucking way! I just want to go home, hide under a cover and never leave the house again.

We're in a backstreet in Umeda, the shopping and entertainment district nearest to my house. Neon flashes everywhere and labyrinthine underground arcades and passage ways run several levels underneath us. We're in a group at the doorway to an izakaya. The football boys are huddled together in an assortment of mismatched match gear, oversize bags slung over their shoulders, I'm shoehorned into a tiny, ancient wheelchair, knees somewhere up around my nose. Jun has borrowed it from some kindly department at the Council Offices. It's perfectly functional but not quite the space age fashion accessory I had been hoping for.

The problem is clear to us all. The izakaya, chosen through a Venn diagram of price, location and reputation, is in the basement, down a dauntingly steep staircase with not an elevator in sight. There's no possible way I can do stairs in the chair. The few times Jun's taken me out somewhere curbs have been scary enough. I'm not fat but me and an awkward chair are a lot for a little Japanese girl to manoeuvre. I've been practising on my stairs at home but I've not yet made it all the way up. These stairs are longer and steeper. This is my special evening, a celebration of me. Coupled with the fact that I'm physically incapable of playing football anymore I'm going back to England in a week. I'll never see these guys again. This is my "soubetsukai"[23]. It won't work very well if I can't get in. No one from the team has thought to ask me what I need and I'm not yet used enough to "New Matt" that I know that I can't afford to be circumspect about my needs.

A team meeting is convened but I am excluded. I sit, wedged in my wheelchair, embarrassed at my existence. A few of these guys - Moriguchi-san, Hashimoto-san, Baba-san, Makoto-kun – had been to visit me in the hospital but a lot of the other guys I hadn't seen since my stroke. The last interaction I had with them was idle banter between games and desperately trying to find a common ground between words I understood in Japanese and words that could possibly describe their jobs. I knew Makoto-kun for 5 years and never really had a clear idea what he did to enable him to acquire all that flashy football kit. I'm just ashamed to be such a problem. There's no sense of being let down or wondering why the restaurant doesn't allow me access. A year after this I would be able to indulge my righteous indignation on the manager, stand up for myself even if I not great at actually standing up, but today I'm just mortally embarrassed of myself. Somehow this is all my fault.

Moriguchi-san is appointed as spokesman and steps forward. He doesn't speak much English but his Japanese combined with hand

---

[23] 送別会 – a farewell party. Everybody makes a speech and gets drunk. A 歓迎会 (kangeikai – welcome party) is almost identical and just as obligatory. No company, department, university society or sports team would be operating correctly if they didn't provide one.

gestures is easy enough to understand – they want to carry me down the stairs. This thought terrifies me. I don't really trust people to look after me with the same care I'd look after myself. But what can I really do? I'm so used to my movements being controlled by someone else and so unwilling to cause a scene. I'm pushed to the lip of the entrance and I stand warily. Four of the guys arrange their arms cradle-like behind me. Moriguchi-san and Hashimoto-san behind my shoulders, Yamamoto-san and Nakamura-san take the legs. Down the stairs we go, slowly at first but gradually a little more confidently. A human body between four people isn't actually that heavy when you think about it. My heart heads back down to my stomach and I start to relax. I let myself be taken care of by these gruff, kindly men. Our grunts turn to giggles and I'm a little disappointed by how quickly we get to the bottom. Baba-san follows with my folded-up wheelchair. I've brought my stick and I'm able to shuffle round to our table and sit cross-legged on the floor in front of the low table. I could never do the Japanese kneeling thing for very long anyway so there's no difference this time.

The meal is a strictly time-controlled success. We can eat or drink all we like for two hours and we take that as a challenge – tempura, karaage[24], sashimi, Asahi Super Dry and exotically coloured cocktails. I pretended not to notice as a futsal ball was passed round and signed as a gift to me and I pretended to understand the heartfelt messages expressed in characters I couldn't really read. People had made the effort – T-shirts with the kanji for "samurai", cuddly toys of my favourite manga characters and even a rising sun headband that I fixed round my forehead to much hilarity. This incongruous bunch of blokes, from early 20's to early 40's, some rich, some poor, some single, some

[24] 唐揚げ– Japanese fried chicken.

married with kids, wanted to give me things to remember them by. I barely knew a few of them but everyone had contributed something. The night was over far too soon and we decanted into the still steam-breath making March evening. The trip back up the stairs accomplished with blasé brio now that we all had a skinful inside us.

I didn't want to be anymore trouble so I started saying my goodbyes, expecting to be left alone. I lied that I was going to call a taxi to get home (in fact I was going to call Jun to come and retrieve me the moment everyone was out of earshot) but the guys wouldn't hear of it. Bandana still in place we careered mob handed back to Nakatsu. People took turns to push my wheelchair, like elder siblings desperate to push the little baby's pram. It must have taken half an hour to get back home but no one ducked out midway. We laughed and straggled along, past the subway station and under the bridge. Jun was stood silhouetted in the doorway as I arrived laden with gifts in plastic bags. Moriguchi-san had even remembered a present for her, a glove puppet of her favourite comic book space frog. Hand over safely accomplished my football team disappeared into the night. We stood into the doorway as their farewells echoed under the railway bridge, lingering long after we lost sight of them.

Chapter 28

March 28th/28th March 2008 – 7 months and 3 weeks since the crippling

Amsterdam Airport Schiphol, Amsterdam, Netherlands

I hate transit wheelchairs. They're the ones with little wheels at the back so you can't move yourself. You're powerless, at the mercy of someone else's mercy. I can see that a lot of people who borrow wheelchairs at the airport are older and perhaps need pushing about but would it kill them to have a couple of self-propelling big back-wheel chairs? I've just spent 14 hours in Economy on a plane from Osaka and I could do with some exercise. Instead I'm immobile in a chair being pushed by a member of the airport staff. Hand luggage, duty free plastic bags and stick are piled awkwardly on my lap. The guy deposits us by an island of chairs next to a concession offering massages, reassures me he'll come and get me in good time for our flight to Birmingham. Jun looks tired as she sits down on one of the chairs. I unwind myself from the wheelchair and totter over to the seats and to join Jun. She offers up a weak, non-committal smile and then goes to sleep.

I'm too tired to sleep. Instead I stand up, retrieve my stick and circumnavigate the island a couple of times. It feels good to be unfurled but I'm so tired and shaky that I'm scared I'll fall and disturb Jun. She needs a rest. I sit back down. I'm so tired. One moment my eyelids are drooping uncontrollably the next I'm unstoppably fidgety, a seated spastic dance. I'm not helped by the involuntary body shakes. These have taken residence in my jaw now. The ones there don't stop as quickly as those in my arm or leg and are consequently the most wearing and the scariest. The bottom half of my face wobbling for up to half an hour at a time. When this comes on just existing is exhausting. It feels like aluminium in my veins, mercury under my tongue. How am I supposed to control anything anywhere if I can't even control myself? I'm so tired and sad. So this is how my life has turned out? I want to wake Jun up and start an argument. I have nothing to argue with Jun about but I'd like to share my pain with someone else however tangentially. I glance down at the Paul Smith watch. It's still set to Japanese time. It was the middle of the night at home in Nakatsu, early evening here. I hoped our next door neighbour Kato-san had remembered to feed Sai.

I never wanted to leave Japan but, as the months passed, it became clear that I would never be able to cope there anymore. I was entitled to benefits as Jun's husband but I wouldn't have had any idea how to go about claiming them. I wanted to go back to work but kind of thing was I really going to be able to do? My boss was keen for me to carry on. He wanted to arrange my schedule so all the schools I worked at were close to a train station. That was a nice idea but I couldn't walk *to* the station in the first place so it wasn't really an option. The job market for gaijin in Japan is incredibly limited – teaching English, modelling or finance (if your company sends you out there from the West). I really needed something I could do from home, whatever that was. What if I needed to go to hospital as an outpatient? Neither of us could drive and Jun worked full-time. I couldn't possibly get anywhere on my own. I can't really read Japanese or work out what's going on in a phone call too well. I had a vague sense of how much help I would need from "The Man" but I wouldn't be able to deal with the simplest piece of communication from him. No, the whole thing was an impossibility. Better I go back to England and fling myself on my parents' doorstep.

So Jun had booked us flights and handled all the disabled flying stuff. There were multiple forms to fill in and doctors to be tracked down. The airline was keen to make sure I was looked after appropriately but also keen to make sure that they were legally covered in case the air pressure caused my head to explode at 30,000 feet. My parents had sent us some money to sort things out. Jun had been amazingly organised. We sorted through books and CD's and sent parcels of stuff back to the UK. She and Sai were moving back in with her parents so she organised the repairs needed to get the house decent enough to give back to the landlord. Sai liked to scratch so she took care of getting door frames smoothed out and fusama doors repapered. A house worth of tatami mats were replaced. The plan was that she would stay in Japan for six months to sort her visa out. Also, if Sai was going to avoid the long, expensive months of quarantine he had to have a microchip inserted under his skin and then be certified disease free for six months. Only then would he be issued with a "Pet Passport" that allowed him seamless entry into the UK. Jun was coming back with me now but she was only staying a few days.

I always knew that I would leave Japan one day but I didn't want it to be like this, tail between my legs, head bowed in defeat. All longer-term foreigners in Japan are issued with a "Gaijin Card", a piece of photo I.D. you are supposed to carry with you at all times. It shows your visa status and proves you have the right to be there. When you finally leave you hand it in at the airport. At the airport I was ushered through a special wider Customs and Immigration channel. My passport was checked and my gaijin card retrieved. The customs official double-checked that I was going home for good.

"I'm going home for eternity" I said in Japanese rather dramatically to the guy. This was mostly because I didn't know the Japanese for "permanently" but it pretty much mirrored how sorry I was feeling for myself. The life I loved was over for eternity. I had lost and here I was, stale and disjointed, in an airport in Holland.

Two men arrived to load me onto the next flight. They seemed nice guys, young and open-minded, impressed that I had spent so long over there and that I spoke the language. They would have assumed that I'd done all this stuff on top of coping with my disability. They didn't see how fresh and infected the wound of my disability was. How would they know? I wasn't date stamped. Now, on top of everything, I felt like a fraud, not even a lifetime crip. We were getting on the plane from the outside this time. I had to climb the stairs into the cabin. I was terrified. I hadn't dared to go up a full flight of stairs since my stroke. Now it was a daunting flight up into a plane on a runway. It was cold and gusty. Snow started to fall and the wind was blowing directly into my face. Unsteadily I began the long, upward trudge into the plane. Right foot up a step, left foot drags up to join it. A brief moment of respite and readjustment and then the next step. The two airport guys positioned themselves front and back of me ready to catch or manhandle me as the situation required. My head swims as I raise it and try to look around. My legs are full of water, choppy and unreliable. One foot in front of the other. I'm losing my breath. One of the airport guys asks if I need to be carried. I haven't got breath spare to speak to him so I just keep stumbling on. I catch my left foot on the edge of a step. I stumble and grasp the rail even tighter. The cabin door slowly nears. The inside looks warm and safe. I keep going, scared to stop. Bursting up the last few steps I tumble into the cabin, dropping my stick and leaning against a welcoming wall for support. A stewardess leads me to my seat and I do an emergency landing into it.

We're the first passengers on and fellow travellers begin to filter down the aisles. I don't want to do this. I don't want to do any of this. I lose control. Tired tears roll down my cheeks and I sob. I never lose control in public and here I am in full view of everyone one. How often do you see a middle-aged man bawl in public? People watch me surreptitiously. Jun holds my hand and dries my tears but I can tell she's embarrassed. I'm not even hugely upset about something in particular. It's just the tsunami of *everything* choosing that particular over-tired moment to crash over my shores. After a minute or two I regain a sniffly sort of composure. The plane takes off. Soon we are landing at Birmingham. My parents meet us and ferry us back to their little village. They've lived there for years but I have never spent longer than a holiday there. I try to imagine when or how I might get back to Japan again. I can't. My new existence is beginning. It will be worse than I can ever imagine.

Part 6

Chapter 29

20th June 2008 – 1 year and 10 months since the crippling

Barrow upon Soar, Leicestershire, England

"I know how you feel." my dad attempts to sound conciliatory.

Five words. That's all. Five stupid words. Five thoughtless words. No one had ever said those words to me since the stroke but here he is. We're in the kitchen – me and my mum and dad. I'm on one side of the room, stick in hand, leaning against the dresser for support. I'm probably crying, red-faced and blotchy, short of breath and struggling to speak in sentences. Arm will be shaking uncontrollably, treacherously. My dad is at the other side of the room by the sink and dishwasher. My mum is sat at the kitchen table.

I've been back from Japan a few months. It'd be fair to say that I'm not taking it very well. Food is wrong. Not enough rice and I've lost my favourite pair of chopsticks. I've managed to get back into the belly of the NHS and I'm getting two physio sessions a week and the odd visit to a consultant. That and non-time difference televised football is, essentially, my life. Jun came back with me and stayed a few days but is now back in Japan with promises to return for good in a few months. We Skype every day but I have so little to talk about that it's hard work. There are a hundred good and sensible reasons why living here is the right thing to do but I often can't think of any of them. Here doesn't feel like home anymore. I miss Jun awfully. I don't have any friends locally. I don't have that many friends in this country anymore. Often I'll go several days without leaving the house and the only people I speak to on a daily basis are my parents. Not that I really speak that much. Aside from logistical information through pursed lips I try not to communicate. I try to be tough for everyone but after a point it all comes tumbling down like it has today and I spend the day sobbing and shouting. I know that none of this is anybody else's fault and I don't want to impinge on their lives. I've chosen to absent myself for so many years that I can't expect just to crash-land back into them. I'm trying to deal with this on my own but often and often unexpectedly the sides split and teary innards flop onto the floor. I have a terrible desire to keep everything private. I immediately switch to Japanese if my mum ever comes in while I'm skyping Jun even if we're just talking about the weather.

I'm in suspended animation. I have no idea what I'm going to do with the rest of my life. I have no idea if my life expectancy is that of a normal person or if I should be preparing for an early death. Strangely this old person's illness seems to have trapped me in adolescence. Here I am living at home with parents who just don't understand me, festering in my bedroom all day, directionless and without motivation. I'm lucky that I've got parents that I can go back to but for someone who's been living independently for nearly twenty years it's nigh on impossible. Weekday mornings would involve trying to be at the breakfast table for 9am. There was usually no reason why I needed to be there at that time but I wanted to seem OK. I knew lying in bed all day was a sign of depression and I didn't want to give anybody a reason to have to express concern about me. That would involve a conversation that I would be unable to participate in. I was pretty sure I was depressed but I didn't want to *seem* depressed to anybody else.

After breakfast I would fill a travel mug with coffee and awkwardly take it upstairs. It had to be a commuting cup thing because I couldn't keep anything lid-less steady enough. The only way I could do this was to place the cup on the furthest step I could reach, let go and follow it up myself clinging on to the banister for support. Once I had caught up with the mug the process would begin again. This was pretty undignified but at least I got a hot drink to my desk.

From there the day yawned endlessly in front of me. I was up but I had nothing to do. I would passively surf the internet or listen to music. Neither gave me much joy. Government departments who should have given me money didn't give me money because they didn't believe that I was back in England for good. I was but I wished I wasn't. It didn't really matter. All I would have done with the money is buy stuff I didn't want from the internet anyway. Sometimes I tried to read but wrestling a book into open-paged submission with one hand often seemed more trouble than it was worth. In the afternoons I would often take to my bed. I rarely slept but tended to stare unblinking at the ceiling in utter incomprehension and horror at what my life had become. Sometimes I cried but only when the house was empty or my parents were in another room and too far away to hear.

On days when I went out I would have to put on my "boot"[25]. I was slightly less reliant on this now than I was in Japan. I could handle midnight trips to the toilet but I still wouldn't dare to leave the house

---

[25] Having got mine in Japan I'd never really got to know a proper name for it. Later I found out that it was called an A.F.O. or Ankle Foot Orthotic.

without it on. My ankle drop is still really bad but this still seems to be an overkill solution, bomb the whole house to destroy the cockroach inside. Why does it need to cover my foot and go up as far as my knee if it's just supposed to be supporting my ankle? Anonymous and off-white I'd tried to personalise it with some "Hysteric Glamour" stickers that Jun had had lying about but I'm not fooling anyone – it's antiseptic and orthopaedic looking. Still I dutifully strapped it on whenever I left the house, terrified of an unknown consequence. When it got too cold for even socks and open toes on my feet I'd graduated from my Japanese Birks into two pairs of Crocs. They did a job but looked unutterably crap. Even with all my aids and accoutrements walking was difficult. I couldn't walk more than 100 yards. In the boot my left leg was heavy and stiff. Every step meant a straight-legged jolt up the bone as my knee locked rigid. It didn't hurt as much as it was unpleasant and ungainly. The stick, the boot, the limp, the chair, the RADAR key, the stilted speech, the immobile left hand, the living with your parents at 36 – I'm completely different from everybody else I know or come into contact with.

I'm a grown man used to running his own life and schedule but now I can't get anywhere by myself. A physio appointment date needs to be coordinated against my mum's commitments before it can be finalised. It's humiliating in a million tiny ways. I don't go anywhere alone. I was a man but at some point I have become a child again. I have no control. At a hospital entrance dad pushes me up a ramp without asking if that is what I want. I scream at him to let me decide when I want some help and not to lay hands on me without checking that it's ok. One Sunday we meet up with my sister, her husband and their little son for lunch at a pub in the Peak District. Our two cars pull up in the designated meet-up car park, me in the back seat of my parents' car and my two year old nephew in the back seat of the other car. We make eye contact and he waves at me. I'm not in a child seat but the parallel feels crushingly obvious. With nothing but the best intentions my self-image is ground into dust. I feel that because I was out of sight on the other side of the world for so long that people think I've always been like this. I have no control over my life, over what I have for tea, what snacks I eat, what beer I drink or how I decorate my room. The situation overwhelms but is also terrifyingly mundane. I'm in the eye of the storm being batted from place to place at the same time as I'm becalmed on a featureless sea.

Nobody talks to me about the stroke and no one talks to me about my life in Japan. I don't really try to. I can't cope with positivity and chivvying up. I'm beyond silver linings and sunny sides. If I could walk perhaps I'd try that side of the street. I don't talk about things because I don't want to hear what I think people would say. My life is a sick joke and I wish I was dead. There doesn't seem to be much anyone could say that would affect that.

This is fine until someone does try to engage. This morning my parents have been trying to talk to me about my "plans" for the last 15 minutes. I have no "plans". I don't even understand how the concept of "plans" could possibly relate to me. The right to make plans was stolen from me on the morning of the 6th of September 2007.

"Do you think you'll go back to university?" my mum asks not unreasonably, "You'll need to get going on an application pretty sharpish if you're going to get sorted for this year."

"Or are you thinking about getting back to work?" asked my dad," Maybe doing something with your Japanese?"

Thinking about a job or studying just seemed miles away. Something a different person could do. How would I even get there? I'm in bits. I can't imagine any kind of a situation where I could be of service to anyone or anything. I need people to do things for me now. Before I could even think about doing anything constructive I would have to reconstruct my constituent parts, put myself back together.

Then my dad said it –

"I know how you feel" the words hung in the air while I caught and digested them.

I lost control completely.

"How could you have any fucking idea how I fucking feel!" I attempted to scream. I was sobbing now. Tears hitting the floor as my head throbbed with frustration. It seemed ridiculous to me. Where I was nowadays was so extreme and unprecedented. So beyond the experience of anything anyone we knew had ever encountered. How could anyone possibly have any idea how I felt? Most days *I* didn't have much idea how I felt but I knew that anybody else wouldn't be able to imagine 1% of it.

"I'm living in hell". The sobs made me virtually unintelligible.

I couldn't cope anymore. Spluttering and coughing through the tears I attempted to storm up to my room. It's hard to storm with a stick and a hobble. The stairs were a problem. I have to go up slowly, keeping a tight hold of the banister. My mum followed me to the bottom of the stairs. She was angry now.

“**GET DOWN HERE AND LISTEN TO US**” she yelled in that “I demand obedience” voice I remembered from childhood. I carried on into my room and flung myself on the bed. None of us were being intentionally mean. We just didn’t possess the tools to talk to each other like a group of adults. I slowly calmed down and my breathing got back to normal. I thought about how we could make up. I had physio tomorrow. I needed a lift.

Chapter 30

18th June 2008 - 10 months since the crippling

Barrow upon Soar, Leicestershire, England

I'll never see Jun again. I'll never see Sai again. I'll never go to Japan again. I'll never have a family. I'll never own a house. I'll never drive a car again. I'll never ride a bike again. I'll never wake up with my whole body working. I'll never sing a song again. I'll never badly impersonate an accent again. I'll never play football again. I'll never get drunk again. I'll never work a full-time job again. I'll never play Grand Theft Auto: Episodes from Liberty City. I'll never change a ceiling light bulb. I'll never be able to hold the phone in one hand and write a message with the other. I'll never walk outdoors without a stick again. I'll never climb Beacon Hill again. I'll never meaningfully kiss a woman again. I'll never sleep with someone again. I'll never have sex with someone again. I'll never visit an onsen again. I'll never ride a rollercoaster again. I'll never wear sandals again. I'll never go bowling again. I'll never wake up in the morning looking forward to the day.

I've got a lot of things to feel bad about. I need my wits about me not to be suffocated, not to be submerged under the weight of my regret, the crushing sense of unfairness. Even if I was in top mental condition all this would be a huge challenge. In my case depression came to stay when I was in a pretty bad place already. If ever there was a time I needed to be able to look on the bright side – this was it. Depression robbed me of even the slightest chance of seeing anything other than the absolute, soul-ground-down-into-the-mud misery of the new me. There were no shafts of light anywhere. It was an unending expanse of pitch-black darkness. I needed all the mental strength I had. I had none.

I cry everyday. Always in private, careful to be inaudible. Having to talk about the desolation of my life with anyone but my therapist is a mortifying thought. I'm a 37 year old male, a product of a single sex private education. We're just supposed to cope. We're not programmed to talk about feelings but I have more than enough feelings for one person and I can't keep them bottled in successfully anymore these days. Great heaving sobs rack my body, tears run down my cheeks and snot bubbles out of my nostrils. My breathing is all wrong. I wretch, almost vomiting my salty sadness. A tense, scary headache is the aftermath but there is no sense of relief. As quickly as I "let it all out" it's recycled back inside. There's never any sense of being done with tears. Just a "same time tomorrow then" feeling of inevitable reoccurrence. Any activity that gives me a moment for silent, private contemplation is liable to set me going. My teardrops mingle with the water in the shower, blur my eyesight as I attempt physiotherapy exercises on my bed and drip onto the remote control as I watch television late at night.

As careful as I am my dad catches me howling one night. Normally they watch telly in one room and I in another so they can't really hear me. He's popped out to the toilet and my whimpering is pretty unavoidable. I think that particular night I was missing Jun and scared that I would lose her. I'm lying on my bed, face damp and chest heaving. Despite my reticence there's no way I can avoid talking to my Old Boy. I tell him I'm scared I'm going to be alone for the rest of my life. This seems like a self-evident truth to me but he disagrees. He has to. He's my father. He's not permitted to be pessimistic about his offspring. That's how it works – parents have to think the best of their children. I must be pushing this to the limit. He tries –

"Don't worry, Matt. Everything will be all right, you'll see."

"Don't give up. Just try to keep going."

I can't work out if he genuinely believes this, is absolutely unable or unwilling to contemplate failure for one of his kids, or is trying to encourage me to struggle on despite all the evidence to the contrary. This is part of the problem – I don't think anyone, especially me, has any idea what constitutes "success" or "failure" anymore. What really is acceptable? I know my parents still hold out a hope of me getting physically better but I've no faith. These just sound like empty platitudes to me but what is my dad supposed to really say? What is he supposed to do? What am I supposed to do? As much as admitting defeat and giving up is a survival strategy for me it must be unbearable for him to see. Eventually I'm calmer. My eyes are still red-rimmed and a toxic headache is brewing but I'm back in control of myself at least. My father makes one last attempt to reach out –

"Why don't you come down and watch telly with me and your mum?"

I appreciate the offer but I can't take them up on it. I'm not a child. I'm in my late 30's. Spending time with my parents should be a holiday treat not how I habitually spend my evenings. Sitting with them, watching TV with them, eating with them – it all reminds me that this used to be the exception rather than the norm. It's not their fault, of course, but their constant presence in my day-to-day life reinforces my infantilization and sense of powerlessness.

This isn't like a bereavement or a break-up. Time doesn't heal this. There's no solution – hate your job? Get a new job. Hate your partner? Get divorced. Hate your post-stroke life? Don't have a stroke. Unless someone invents time travel I'm totally fucked. Depression turns everything into reminders of the life you once had, memory and ash. I spend as much time as possible in the past. Now is too awful to contemplate but the future is worse. The future is too terrifying for words. I can't imagine anything aside from loneliness, poverty, sheltered housing, care workers and losing "me". As awful as it is in many ways, I'm comfortable here with my parents – a meal cooked every night, en suite bathroom and all the Sky channels possible. What happens after they go?

I was 35 when I had my stroke. Assuming nothing happens I have half my life still to go like this and I've got to find *something* to do until I die. I'm careful not to do anything that looks too "depressed" – I don't stay in bed all morning, I shave, I wash, I don't drink too much. I only choose not to leave my room and talk to visitors *occasionally*.

Desperation eventually leads me tearfully to the Doctor's surgery and a prescription for anti-depressants. I'd always resisted them on the grounds that "I needed to feel what I was feeling" or something. Needing to "feel what I was feeling" is a laudable idea but I was feeling too much too intensely and it was stopping me functioning at all. All I was doing was "feeling what I was feeling" 24 hours a day to the exclusion of anything else.

The Citalopram tablets the doctor gives me after I noisily blub in his room are my life-savers, 10mg of calm once a day. I take the tablets last thing at night just before bed. They are tiny, often jumping out of my hand and making a break for freedom under the bed. Not an easy retrieval for a sleepy cripple. Such a little thing makes such a difference. A little bolt of Buddhism that infuses through my whole day. I'm not so crushed by fear of my future that I can't live for today. I'll still think about my next decade but am able to make plans for next week as well. Friends I've seen on other anti-depressants seemed so spaced out, it seemed as though they were simply taking a holiday from their head. I'm still totally aware of what I'm going through but I'm able to face today with out a continual, ever expanding anvil hanging over my head.

I'm lucky in that the first pill I try works perfectly. I start on 20mg but soon find 10mg is enough. I have odd rushes of euphoria, strange echoes of the few times Ecstasy was more MDMA than jaw-clenching sulphate, but no side effects. The rushes feel like whooshing, confetti-in-the-air, huge tumbling piano riffs (all I can compare it to is the massive synth breakdown in "Last Train to Transcentral" by the KLF) but perhaps that is just me. Perhaps this was how "normal" people felt all the time but familiarity dims the euphoria? I didn't remember. Perhaps real, normal life, the life that was lost to me on the 6th of September 2007, was like permanently being on amazing E in the best nightclub in the world in 1989?

Chapter 31

3rd September 2008 – 1 year since the crippling

Barrow upon Soar, Leicestershire, England

The period between getting up and getting showered is my favourite time of day. Even with nothing to fill the day I still set my alarm and get up at 6.30am. It's still dark outside and my curtains are tightly drawn. I'm cocooned in my dressing gown and my glasses are perched on the end of my nose as I peer at the laptop screen. I like this time of day because no one will disturb me and no one can expect me to be doing anything constructive. I'm quiet and have no music on so I like to imagine no one else in the house knows I'm up. Plus all my websites will have new content to read – new news, new record reviews and the latest transfer gossip. This is one of the few times in a day when I can say that I'm doing exactly the same thing as I would when I lived in Japan. I always liked to give some internet time before I went to work. My browsing took me to the newspaper and the picture of the oversize, near-naked pair of men caught my eye. It was incongruous – like part of my past life invading my present. I remembered the first time I had gone to the sumo. It was my first year in Kyoto and I remember the fuggy Municipal Gymnasium, the texture of the rice straw under my palm and the sight of bodies flung with full force into each other repeated hour upon hour.

We'd crammed ourselves onto the tatami mats assigned to us. Too many of us in a cramped space. Six oversize whities of varying shapes and genders. Me and some work colleagues including the guy who can speak Japanese well enough and is senior enough that he can sort out the tickets and, after a fashion, us. The mats are designed to be knelt on in the Japanese style but few of us can manage this for any length of time before we desperately need to unwind our legs and all end up taking up twice our allotted space. Curse my overgrown, graceless Gaijin body! We are all assigned a cushion but these are so thin as to be little use for anything except arcing towards the ring at the end of the day.

I don't know why I am here aside from it being something that you *should* do while you are in Japan – attend a sumo tournament is definitely on the "to do" list. Apparently it's very popular and often sold out but a few "first come-first served" tickets for that day's bouts are released first thing in the morning. We've got to Osaka early enough to snag ours but it's involved an early start and a crowded commuter train from Kyoto. Still a sugary Mister Donut refuelling stop keeps me going. We settle into our spot. Getting in early means we're going to see a lot of sumo. We're here at about 10am but the headline bouts don't start until around 4. Guys just starting out or nose-diving down the strictly ranked divisions battle it out to little audience interest. We're so far away from the dohyo[26] that we can barely see what is going on. It's just two half-naked fight guys thundering into each other. After each bout the referee would indicate the winner. Often we couldn't tell why someone had won or lost. We began betting coppers on who would win. While becoming very little the

[26] 土俵 - Ring where the fighting goes on.

wiser it was a great day. Aside from the actual wrestling there was so much spectacle – wrestlers slamming their feet down and chucking salt about before each bout, the ceremonial entrance that each group of wrestlers make before they start, parading round the ring in ornate brocade aprons. The wrestlers walk through the crowd from the changing rooms to the ring. Stand in the corridor next to the locker room and you can get a close up view of the wrestlers going in and going out. From our vantage point in the hall they looked like big guys but up close they were immense. I imagined that I could feel the floor shake as they passed by.

Gradually the room filled out and the air around us became an uncomfortable mix of sweaty steam and cigarette smoke. The atmosphere rose as the last fight of the day began. Fighters fought in reverse order – the highest ranked did battle last. A huge Japanese guy shoved another huge Japanese guy out of the ring. Either this made everyone happy or it made everyone sad because they frisbee-d their cushions towards the centre. We joined in, giggling and exuberant. The day was done. I had some out-of-focus long distance shots of sumo wrestlers for the album and a "Japanese Experience" ticked off my list. Now to stalk a geisha. I went home tired but content and still pretty ignorant about what I'd been watching.

Then a funny thing happened. Over the next year or two I got genuinely, sincerely into sumo. I don't quite know how it happened. Sumo is not a young person's sport. It held no appeal whatsoever to any of the guys I played football with. Jun feigned interest for my benefit but I saw that she couldn't really care less and that I was pretty much on my own. I felt a little guilty. Being "into" sumo was a quintessentially crap gaijin thing to do – "Look at me! I'm so integrated and deeply immersed in Japanese culture that I love sumo". I hated all that pseudo-anthropology. I didn't have a theory about what the Japanese were like. Well not one that I ever shared with anyone.

It happened by accident. I often got home a few hours before Jun. Me and Sai would usually flop in front of the telly for a while after I got back from work. Sumo is on *a lot*. 6 two week tournaments a year. The tournaments run everyday for those two weeks and everyday is televised live. NHK, the Japanese equivalent of the BBC, provides an English commentary as well as Japanese. In effect there is live sumo on telly on one day in four. I saw *a lot* of sumo and slowly began to understand what was going on and to recognise the contestants. I started to understand why people had won or lost. There was a delicious specialised vocabulary to learn - yokozuna[27], kimarite[28], tachiai[29]. I began to recognise and root for particular wrestlers – Takamisakari – strange smacking himself warm up technique and Eurobeat fan, Kotomitsuki – gentlemanly and noble but perhaps lacking the killer instinct, mushashimaru, the Samoan yokozuna who didn't seem that interested, Asashoryo, the Mongolian who seemed to want to win at any cost.

I grew to love Sumo. Rushing home from work to catch the bouts. I loved that it had meaning beyond pure sport. A standard of behaviour is expected aside from just winning. Great champions meant more than just winners. A certain standard of behaviour was expected. When a wrestler finally retired a special ceremony was held to formally

---

[27] 横綱 – highest ranking sumo wreslers.

[28] 決まり手 - the particular technique used to win a bout.

[29] 立ち合い - the initial charge at the start of the bout.

cut off his top knot. It is a sport intrinsically tied up with Shinto-ism and ritual. Every little thing has relevance and a significance. The salt the wrestlers chuck around at during their elongated warm ups is meant to purify the ring before they defile it, it's a classic example of a build-up and release. The days main fights could be shown on telly in five minutes but the ceremonies, warm ups and formalities would take hours. Wrestlers could spend up to 15 minutes tossing salt, doing the crouching sideways stamp thing, drinking the "water of power" and attempting to psych out their opponent. When they finally got down to fighting it was often over in a matter of seconds but the anticipation was incredible. Foreplay is important. I knew the stories. That referee was a retired wrestler who had a lot of potential but had been too short to be admitted into the ranks so they'd surgically inserted a lump under his scalp to give him the required extra inches. The scandal of the young wrestler hazed at his training camp who later died. The yokozuna who claimed to be injured but was then caught playing in a charity football match in Mongolia.

Sumo was a lifesaver while I was in hospital. It gave the day some structure and gave me something to look forward to, a tiny, tiny reason to be glad that I wasn't at work. I'd usually finish my rehab by mid-afternoon and then settle down, headphones in, to watch the bouts. The final head-to-head was usually at about the time I was called to dinner but they had a telly in the dining room so I could watch and it gave me something to talk to the oldsters about. Life seemed even duller when a tournament wasn't on.

The newspaper article that had induced my reverie was about the latest trouble to befall the world of sumo. It must have been pretty serious to garner news coverage outside Asia. Sumo's reputation was being regularly battered during my time following it but this was worse. Two Russian wrestlers had tested positive for marijuana. Japan has a much more hard-line attitude to recreational drugs than most developed countries and this was a major scandal. As the months passed things were going to get much worse: Eventually two dozen wrestlers were suspended for suspected gambling offences (gambling is strictly controlled in Japan). Kotomitsuki, one of my sumo idols and a seeming keeper of the noble flame, has admitted to being extorted by a member of the yakuza who threatened to expose his illegal gambling. He's later expelled from sumo permanently and denied a retirement ceremony. My other hero was Mongolian bad-boy Asashoryu. He was forever ruffling feathers with the sumo authorities. His lack of reverence for the sumo traditions equalled only by his strength and will to win. The article went on to say that he had been encouraged to "retire" at the ludicrously young age of 29. He had broken a man's nose in a drunken brawl outside a nightclub. I was gutted. Gutted for the wrestlers who had been trained to do nothing but fight since childhood and were now cut asunder from their quintessence. Gutted for myself as well. Japanese life had had the temerity to move on in the 2½ years since I had left and my carefully constructed image of a fantasy Japan where everything was better and trustworthy was being destroyed. Cast adrift from another of those little things that make up my identity. Not only were things that I had thought were secure crumbling about me but I didn't even know anything about it anymore. Nothing and no one did what it was supposed to. Rikishi[30] were mutating and so was I. I couldn't even keep my imaginary worlds consistent. Even my past was becoming sullied.

---

[30] 力士 – sumo wrestlers.

There was nothing I could rely on anymore. Everything was changing and no part of it was for the better.

Chapter 32

12th November 2008 – 1 year and 2 months since the crippling

Birmingham, West Midlands, England

Today is the day. I was so excited that I had barely slept the night before. It was the night before Christmas. In fact it was more like New Year's Eve. Today is the start of a new year or even a new life. Today is the day I get a big piece of freedom back. Freedom of movement is a key tenet to most definitions of independence and liberty. It's Clause 1 of Article 13 of the United Nations Universal Declaration of Human Rights issued in 1948. I don't have it. Some times I don't leave the house for days at a time. There's very little popping to the shops or nipping out for a quick pint in my life nowadays.

But that is all about to change. Today is the day that I get my driving license back. Well I don't actually get it handed back to me. There's no ceremonial handing back of my license. There's no sterling silver, velvet lined case opened to reveal a credit card-sized bit of plastic lying inside and winking lasciviously at me. But today could be the day. It's The Regional Driving Assessment Centre in Birmingham who will decide if I'm capable of driving an adapted car and then make a recommendation to the DVLA in Swansea. Then, after all the necessary bureaucratic cogs have clanked, I should get my driving license back and then I'll have access to the sweet "cars for cripples" scheme run by the government – choice of no deposit cars, free servicing, free insurance and RAC membership. It's a good deal. It occasionally occurs to me that I don't actually have very many places to go but that seems a minor inconvenience more than anything else. Going for a cup of coffee at the motorway services at Leicester Forest East and exchanging small talk with the spotty, hair-netted teenager behind the till seems pretty exciting to me.

I've been to this industrial estate in Birmingham before a few months ago. The assessment centre performed an initial check on my needs. I'd never even seen an adapted car before so driving one was a bit of a shock. I'd trundled nervously around the industrial estate where the centre was situated desperately trying to watch the road and work out the unfamiliar one-handed controls at the same time. I was beginner-inept but the assessor reassured me that I just needed a few lessons to get used to it all and I would be fine. He recommended the British School of Motoring and arranged for me to come back for another check in a few months.

I got home, dutifully called B.S.M. and booked some lessons. Pretty soon I was pottering around Leicestershire apprehensive and hesitant behind an adapted steering wheel.

Working a car around my non-working leg is no problem. Driving an automatic only requires one foot. I was used to gears but this was an inconvenience more than anything else. I could reach across myself to put the handbrake on with my right hand. It was ungainly but perfectly do-able. Operating the rest of the car with one hand is more of a challenge. They fit a knob to the steering wheel allowing you to navigate one handed. Attached to the knob are a bunch of buttons to operate indicators, lights, windscreen wipers and so on. That all sounds relatively simple doesn't it? It didn't seem to be. It could have been performance anxiety – this was not a normal kind of test. It wasn't about getting a job, a qualification or a place at university. This was an exam to get my life back. If I passed then I could go places – visit the few friends I had left, think about being able to get to a job or do a college course. I dreamt about picking Jun up from the airport by myself next time she came to visit. She didn't drive so this would be something I could do for her, something that she would need me to do for her, a skill I would possess, a service I could perform for her. I could make myself useful in a very real way.

The controls were hard. I couldn't find the buttons by touch alone. Casting furtive glances away from the road ahead whenever I needed the indicators. Steering seemed harder still. Now that meant to be the easy part – point the car where you wanted to go. Simple. Somehow I just didn't seem to be able to get the car to go where I wanted. I understeered. I oversteered. I drifted towards the central set of white lines. Two hands on a steering wheel makes a nice stable rectangle – torso, two arms and a steering wheel. One arm just doesn't work as well. It wobbles and judders. It's either too stiff or too flexible. Reversing was a nightmare. My neck seemed to have lost some of its ability to rotate at some point. The guy in Birmingham recommended I have about half a dozen lessons, any more and I would be getting ripped off. I think I had about 20.

As the day of the assessment approached the instructor wrote a letter detailing my strengths and weaknesses to give to the assessor and gruffly told me "you'll be ok". I wasn't. My dad took me to Birmingham on the appointed day. Me and the assessor did the necessary paperwork and checked my eyesight was acceptable. He led me out to the comically small car outside. I clambered in and we drove off. I was nervous as hell, disconcerted by not hearing my instructor's constant and mindless prattle in my ear. I was just about blagging it until we got to a T-junction. I thought I had plenty of space to make the turn and squeeze in front of the on-coming car. Turns out I didn't. The assessor slammed down the Dual Control pedals of shame. It was downhill from there. I knew I had failed and I just gave up. At one point the guy had to grab the steering wheel and stop me scraping along the side of a parked van. As I limped the car back into the centre. I already knew the outcome. As I trudged towards the guy's office I passed my dad in the foyer. He gave me a hopeful smile and asked how it had gone.

In the office the guy told me I wasn't able to drive and, worse still, that there wasn't much point trying again unless there was "a significant change" in my condition. This driving tester's medical assessment of my condition was that I had acquired some pretty significant spatial awareness issues at some point over the course of my illness. As he listed my deficiencies I realised that they were pretty much identical to those listed in the letter the B.S.M. instructor had listed. I drifted into the centre of the road and I had some trouble judging gaps but he didn't see these things as a huge problem. The assessor did.

As my dad drove us home he was full of talk of appeals and protests. It was impressively combative but I couldn't join in. I got home and went straight to bed. This felt like the end of my world. The door to the world had been left slightly ajar. Now it had been slammed shut. This was something I had been banking on for the last few months. Life *would* be better when I could drive. The last year had been heartbreak followed by disaster, trauma on top of trauma. Nothing good had happened to me since September 6th 2007. This was going to be different from everything since then. This was an advantage. I'd never been able to afford a car. I'd never even had a license while I was in Japan. This was something I could gain. Something that would be a benefit. This would have been the first tangibly, unequivocally good thing to come from all this *fucking shit*. I could go places without all the usual shenanigans. I could pick people up. I could be useful to other people. I could be of service. Not because I had a huge desire to help anybody else anymore but it gave you some power. People would rely on you. I would have a piece of control. I didn't see how I could do anything when there was no way to get about. That night in bed I couldn't even cry. I was broken.

When I told Jun what had happened. She immediately offered to learn to drive. Learn in Japan and then try to convert her license for the UK roads. A sensible idea but it made it longer still until she appeared here I couldn't expect her to learn to drive overnight. It took time. Everything that happened was unbearable in its own discrete way but then it bled into something else seemingly unconnected and made that even worse – I couldn't drive and that was bad enough in itself but it also meant that me and Jun wouldn't be able to be together for even longer. Nothing was going to be OK ever again.

Chapter 33

13th January 2009 – 1 year and 5 months since the crippling

Barrow upon Soar, Leicestershire, England

Me and Jun normally Skype on a Sunday. Mid-morning for me makes early evening for her. This works quite well – I have nothing to do on but wait for Super Sunday to start and Jun can have a chat before she has tea and a bath. When we were first separated we tried to Skype everyday but it didn't really work. As much as I wanted to keep the connection alive there were only so many ways we could have the same conversation –

"What are you doing for the rest of today, Matt?"

"Nothing. I've got no plans."

"Ok. You just relax and take it easy. That's probably the best thing."

I just didn't have enough chat to sustain daily conversation. I didn't *do* anything. No – that's not true. I was doing a lot of things. Perhaps I just didn't want to talk about them? I went to outpatient rehab at the hospital twice a week and went to see my counsellor weekly. I had started attending a head injury support group every week and this had led me to a continuing education photography course in Leicester. Plus

I was busy doing all the logistical stuff that comes with becoming disabled overnight – trying (and failing) to get my driving license back, almost daily battles with the benefit system and trying to understand just how things had come to *this* and what on earth I was going to do with the rest of my life. I had plenty of things I wanted to talk about but I just couldn't find the words to talk to Jun. To begin with I didn't possess the Japanese vocabulary. We'd never had to talk about these kinds of things. I didn't think Jun would understand if I tried to talk about things in English. We normally used Japanese and I was fairly fluent but I wasn't great at speaking abstractly. I could say that "I lived in hell" but I couldn't really explain why. With no way to expand on it I thought I just sounded like a foot-stamping toddler. But that wasn't the only thing – I still felt that I needed to be tougher. I couldn't just complain all the time. Jun had said that if this had happened to her she "wouldn't have cried as much". I remember when she said that. I was on my back unable to get out of bed. She would leave the hospital and catch the tube home in an hour. I was tormented by the idea that I wasn't strong like Jun. She'd always been tough and I was a bit of a nonce. I was smart but I had no common sense. It had been a running joke in our relationship. She didn't want to hear me whining all the time. Perhaps this whole thing wasn't as bad as it seemed? Perhaps I just needed to accept things? Bad stuff happened everyday. It just happened that today the arrow had pointed to me. What real right had I to complain? If it wasn't me it was someone else and I didn't bitch when it happened to them. I would tough it out. Show Jun that I was I was strong. That she could be proud. This unnatural jaw-thrust-out facade would last for a few months before it collapsed into an inevitable, snivelling heap in front of the webcam.

So I'd changed our daily Skypes to weekly. This gave me a bit longer to come up with the story of the week. I'd even started researching vocabulary trying to find out what "social worker" or "government benefits" were in Japanese. This Sunday was cold and fresh. Life was getting back to normal after the Christmas and New Year upheaval. Jun had sent me some Marc Jacobs aftershave. I didn't really know who Marc Jacobs was but Jun assured me that she was wearing the female version. I liked that – unity through scent. She had also sent me a couple of boxes of that Lisn Autumn Twilight incense that I loved so much. The slightest hint of the scent drifting across my nostrils would instantly transport me back to our rickety home in Nakatsu. I'd got Jun a Tesco gift card. As lame as that sounds she loved Tesco and, crucially, she had to be here to spend it.

This Sunday Jun was busy – out for a drink with Hiromi. We'd normally leave it till the next weekend but this time Jun wanted to talk sooner. We exchanged a few emails and arranged for Tuesday. This was nice – she wanted to talk.

Tuesday rolled around, I logged into Skype and positioned myself in front of the webcam. Jun came on line unusually quickly and made the call. I answered, trying to remember all the topics I had been mentally preparing.

"Hi Jun! How are you?"

"Not great. I need a copy of your passport."

"Oh, Ok. I'll post it to you."

"No I need it quicker. Please can you fax it to me today, Matt?"

There was a strange urgency in her voice I didn't recognise. Sound quality over Skype wasn't great. Jun didn't always sound like I remembered her. I never sounded like how I remembered me.

"Ok, Jun. Why do you need it?"

There were often arcane intricacies of Japanese bureaucracy that I didn't understand. Jun was Padmore now so perhaps they needed proof that I actually existed. For tax or something?

There was a slight pause on the other end of the Internet. Perhaps Jun took a deep breath before the next sentence or perhaps Sai was too heavy on her lap and she repositioned him.

"I need it to get a divorce. I need to go back to being an "Adachi". I need to go to the 'kuyakusho[31]'. Being "Padmore" is too painful. I need your passport."

Jun starts sobbing. She doesn't cry often and I've never heard these sort of sobs before. Single and determined they don't sound like anything I have a connection to anymore. Each time she breaks down she comes back with a renewed perseverance. She needs a photocopy of my passport so she can take it to the council offices tomorrow and use it as proof of my consent to the divorce. She's taken a day off work in readiness. It's just one trip to fill in some forms and it's all done. I remember how easy getting married was.

I'm taken totally by surprise. In the same way that having a stroke was totally unexpected so is this. Anger is rising in me, up my veins and into my skull. I can feel it racing up my arms from my fingers. My right hand

---

[31] 区役所 – local council offices

clenches the mouse. My left arm shakes uncontrollably. We'd never talked about divorce before.

I drag the story out of Jun. She's distant and factual now. Our planets are orbiting separate suns suddenly. I'm angry but trying to get to the bottom of this all. Jun went to see the Moyamoya specialist on the Friday of the week before. Moyamoya is much rarer in non-Asian countries and because of that he told her it wouldn't be safe for her to move away from Japan. Not safe to leave Japan. The UK, here, where I really need to live now, is clearly not "Japan". So Jun can't come here. I can't go there. That's it, then. Simple as that. Our dream, our marriage, destroyed in a sentence. What else did the doctor do that day? Did he inadvertently destroy anybody else's life? His one sentence ruined an already shattered life 6000 miles away. My brain wasn't functioning anymore. There was too much information jostling for space. Jun was scaring me. Each new revelation seemed to end with "so I need your passport". I'm losing control of myself, spluttering at the keyboard, ranting. I'm not really saying anything of any meaning, just raging at the unfairness of it all. I deserve something good. Not this. Not my one true friend leaving me. The lava in my veins spurts.

"I'm not going to send the fucking passport now. Talk to me in one month. February 15th and if you still want it I'll send it to you then. Think about everything!"

You can't really slam down the receiver when you're talking to a screen but I tried. I slammed the cursor onto the red phone symbol on the screen and disconnected mid-sentence. I flung the mouse across the room and it bounced off a chest of drawers. It lay undamaged on the carpet. Even my grand gestures of angst were futile.

I stood up from the computer, flopped ungainly onto the double bed and attempted to regulate my breathing. I'd never thought of the situation like this. Jun's Moyamoya had been around for a few years. She'd spent time in hospital and was taking daily tablets. Her arms sometimes shook and she was not always herself but the doctors didn't do anything particular for her. She had a three-monthly meeting with the specialist but he didn't seem to do anything besides monitor and prescribe new and equally ineffective courses of pills. I could see that it was something that bothered Jun a lot but, really, how serious could something be if you only saw the doctor 4 times a year? The hospital Jun went to was just a few Tube stations away. It was run by one of the world experts on Moyamoya. People travelled from all over Japan to see him. We were lucky to be so near. My work contract had to be renewed annually and I was beginning to make vague noises about us moving here in a year or two but why would we move when Jun was next door to some high-class medical care? I renewed my contract. It was an easy decision. Get Jun's stuff sorted and then move back later. It was simple logic. Nothing more. It wasn't as much of a sacrifice as Jun seemed to think. This was when I still thought that all illnesses were curable. People like us didn't suffer ill-health for any length of time. People like us got better. I knew I couldn't live this slightly student, intransient life for ever. We had to get to England and do proper grown-up, mortgage stuff one day soon but Jun's health was obviously the most important thing.

I'd just assumed that the Moyamoya was just something we'd work around. When it was a bit more under-control Jun would come to England, we'd find a specialist who knew a bit about it and we'd manage the situation. It had never seemed to be a reason why we couldn't move to England. The little that was being done for Jun there could easily be replicated here. Now, with me being ill that was that. I had to go to England and Jun would follow me. Maybe. I was scared that Jun wouldn't want to come. I was a fucking cripple after all – you couldn't blame someone for wanting to flee from me – but I never thought anything else would stop us. Relationships and illnesses always just involved one person getting sick, right? That was how it worked, never both people. People went into hospital to be cured and disabled people always achieved whichever life-affirming, heart-warming challenge they set for themselves.

Me and Jun didn't speak for that month and I gradually calmed down. I understood how things were even as I hated every single part of it. What was the point of being married if you couldn't ever be together? I couldn't expect Jun to ignore the doctor. A worst-case-scenario, he had warned, was that Jun could end up having a stroke. I was a pretty good advert for "Not Having a Stroke". However much he was fucking up the one good thing left in my life he was still the doctor. I'd met him and he'd seemed like a decent man. It was easy for me to imagine him as a Western-hating xenophobe plotter attempting to fuck up the stinky barbarians one man at a time but he was just a doctor. I didn't ever want anything bad to happen to Jun. In a stand-up fistfight between "Matt's happiness" and "Jun's health" she won every time – first round knockout. The awful simplicity of the situation made it easier to take in a way. I couldn't see any other possibilities. I could harangue Jun as much as I liked but I would risk losing a friend. We'd shared too much for that and, anyway, I didn't have a whole heap of friends. A webcam friend is better than no friend at all.

I admit that a big part of this was pride. I had been suddenly emasculated and infantilised but I had had a real life before and I wanted to prove it to people even if they hadn't seen the day-to-day workings of it. Out of my family only Mum and Dad had come to my wedding. Everyone else had met Jun during summer holidays and Christmases but it had always been a bit of a special occasion. Much more "Ooh! Jun's coming to visit. It'll be nice to see her again." rather than just a normal part of any event involving family "Dave&Sue, Matt&Jun and Richard&Emma are all coming." I'd done all this stuff – marriage, lived abroad, travelled to all these amazing countries but I somehow didn't think anyone really believed I'd done any of it. I was just a disability now. Jun would be living proof that I was something else as well.

The month passed and I still didn't want to send the passport over but I knew that it was the right thing to do. There was nothing to be gained by being stupid. As much as I detested the marrow of this situation Jun had showed me so much love before, during and after the stroke. The least I could do was respect her wishes. On the 15th of February I logged onto Skype prepared to tell Jun that I'd do what she wanted. I imagined a terse, awkward conversation but it went along our usual lines -

"Hi Jun. How are you?

"Not too bad, Matt. I've had a cold. How are you?"

The conversation continued in a comfortingly familiar way – Sai was fat, Jun's Mum was a bit mental, she was jealous that we were having roast beef for Sunday lunch and not surprised that Nottingham Forest were losing more matches. I was enjoying having a normal conversation with Jun after our last chat but I was expecting some terrible addendum to every bit of a chat –

"Yeah work is really busy. I'm having to do overtime everyday. Oh, by the way, can you send me the passport please?"

Jun didn't like drama - this is the way she would do it. Talking about something as though it wasn't anything special seemed to make it so for Jun. But nothing came. As we were winding things up she had still said nothing about it. Perhaps she was embarrassed? I felt it was a little rich to expect me to remind her that this was supposed to be the phone call where we finalised our divorce, the divorce that I didn't want to get, but I was set on being tragically noble -

"Ok Jun, Have a nice bath. Shall I send you the passport?"

"Let's talk about it another time, OK? Talk to you next week. Enjoy the football! Byeee!"

That was it. We weren't getting divorced this week. It felt like a small victory for "not being an arse". The next weeks and months of Skype were good. I started some voluntary work at a local primary school and that gave us something new to talk about. We relaxed around each other again. And the idea began to germinate –

This was impossible. Trying to construct a way for Jun to get into my UK life was impossible. Even if she could stay safely stay here what would we do? I couldn't support her. I had my hands full with myself. Jun is an extremely capable person but she wasn't a fluent speaker of English. What would she do for work? Where would we live? Neither of us could drive so how would we get anywhere? If Jun came over here she would be my responsibility. If I let her down I couldn't forgive myself. I was a barely functioning human being on any level. I didn't mind relying on my parents in a hundred different ways and being hell to live with as I went through the psychological trauma of all this. They had to take it - they were family. Jun was family as well but I didn't want to subject her to the tears and tantrums, shouting and silences that seemed to be how I communicated these days.

I hated the idea of casting the last bit of my old life adrift but I liked the idea of taking a bit of pressure off me. This was a challenge I felt I could only fail. I didn't want to let Jun down. She smoothed out so many creases in my Japanese life and I had believed that I would do something similar for her fledging English life. Now I had no faith in being able to do this anymore. Gradually, over a few months, I began to realise that perhaps my marriage was weight I needed to throw from the balloon if I was to have a chance of keeping it up in the air. But I couldn't say the words "I want a divorce". That just seemed too much like giving up on the best thing in my life. As much as I could understand rationally that there was only one way that this could end emotionally I couldn't let go. I still bobbed on the driftwood hoping that the ship would somehow unsink itself and pop back up to the surface while surprised and dripping attendants rearranged the deckchairs.

I was in stasis. There was no room to manoeuvre in any direction. Only one thing that could possibly be done. I ordered a card online and wrote a message to Jun. I told her thanks for everything she had done for me and that the best days of my life were with her. I hope that she would get another boyfriend one day. I know that is going to hurt like no pain I have ever felt but I hope she does. I hope she is able to find some happiness. I hope I can. I photocopied my passport, put the sheet inside and posted it to Japan. Jun got it a week later. On our Sunday Skype she didn't mention it until I brought it up.

"Thanks, Matt. I got it on Thursday. I'll use it when I need to."

I was sadly satisfied that I had done the right thing. Now Jun could do it whenever she wanted to.

Chapter 34

7th October 2009 - 2 years and 1 month since the crippling

Loughborough, Leicestershire, England

So I'm off to my first proper day at university. It's a kind of "will to power" thing. I can now walk far enough to get the two busses I need to get to the college. I can speak well enough to hold a conversation with an understanding listener but I have no confidence about my ability to hold my own in a group conversation or even to be audible. I've heard vague talk of "doing presentations" but I'm trying to block it out.

I have a pretty clear understanding that I have to do something supposedly constructive. Going to university at my hometown college is a perfectly reasonable course of action in Japan but to me it reeks of failure and inadequacy. Not a good starting point but I'm not really in a position to be picky. Extensive road(bus?)-testing over the summer has shown me I can get there and just about manage a bit of a walk once I'm here. I've found the department building and that's just about within my range but they haven't decided exactly where the classes are going to be held. An arbitrary room choice could end up costing me hundreds of quid in taxi fares. It's going to involve a lot of taxis anyway depending on the weather – no running for the bus juggling bag and brolly for me anymore.

These are the strange practical decisions my life revolves around these days. Not "Do I want to go there?" anymore but "Can I get there?" It makes no odds whether it's a better course somewhere else – I couldn't really get anywhere else without a huge load of hassle and expense.

So my choice of course is dictated by what's on offer at Loughborough and what I could possibly do. I settle on "Creative Writing" because it seems likely that I've got a chance of getting on the course, I write a blog (that's kind of "Creative Writing", right?) and writing is something that you can do one-handed and don't need to move about too much for. Bit stupid to be thinking too much about my future but you've got to do something, haven't you? Before when I was busy earning money and living my life doing something like this would never have occurred to me. This is the nearest thing to an opportunity that my stroke has given me so far. An unwanted opportunity maybe but still a chance to do something different that I never expected to be able to try. While this is something I have a vague interest in I would never have chosen to do this if things hadn't turned out the way they did. I recognise that I need something to do. I'm essentially spending my life savings on an "activity", a coat hanger to hang my week on, to give it some shape and hoping that the amorphous blob on my horizon can congeal into something tangibly real and positive. Plus it involves new on-line shopping opportunities – a chain to hang my bus pass round my neck, a smaller version of my old kindergarten teaching work bag, stationery. It's good to have something new to research and order. The bag is designed for San Francisco cycle messengers and is tough and expensive. Most weeks it contains no more than a notebook, a pen and the black overhead cagoule that I never once wear.

I don't have any choice about anything abstract. It's purely practicalities. "Can I afford this?", "Can I manage that?" All the normal choices that a mature student would have to make are alien irrelevancies to me – "Will this fit around my work?", "Will this increase my employability?" – this is all gobbledygook.

I have vague hopes of finagling a social life out of this, students so skint they would jump at the chance of being my complimentary +1 "carer" at the cinema or concerts. Time together driven by necessity would blossom into a genuine friendship. People enticed by the strength and forbearance of my newly forged personality (my counsellor is quite good at convincing me that I'm still capable of doing people stuff like making friends). It turns out that there only five other people on the course – two of them have the temerity to be even older than me and the other three are a good 15 years younger than me. Everyone is perfectly nice and I grow to genuinely like them but, a year later, I'm still spending my evenings in front of the telly as alone as before.

The first seminar is reasonably ok to get to and it passes with little incident. I'm audible, there's somewhere to rest my newly bought notebook and I don't fall asleep. I'm not convincing about "what I want to get from the course" but, then, I don't know myself really. I make a great joke about "Chinatown". I know it was funny because I nicked it from "Flight of the Concords" the night before. It's a few weeks later, after getting to know everyone on the course a bit better, that I realise that it's unlikely that any of them knew what I was talking about. They all seem like they have enough real life stuff going on that they don't have the time or inclination to be need to be the kind of people who watch critically acclaimed Roman Polanski films. They probably hadn't seen it. They all laughed uproariously but I reckon they were just being polite. "Chinatown" may well be one of Polanski's classics but it's a bit boring really, isn't it? I doubt it's getting many first time viewers these days.

The other thing I want accomplish this year is to meet some Japanese people locally. The university is an obvious hunting ground for this. When I was in Japan people would assume you wanted to be friends simply because they were interested in the West or were a bit better at English than the average person. Compatibility or shared interests were not really a consideration. I often felt like a cipher or a stereotype but this was exactly what I was intending to do except in reverse. I can speak Japanese therefore any Japanese people in the vicinity will be irresistibly entranced by my linguistic skills and yearn desperately for my friendship. It hasn't happened so far.

To this end I was excited to hear snippets of Japanese drifting through the marketplace as I hobbled towards my second bus on the way home. There were three of them, two boys and a girl, student young, obviously spending some time at the university. They were naturally cool in the way that only exists over there, all manga hair and Louis Vuitton accessories. They were excitedly taking pictures. I followed the direction of the lens but it all looked dull to my jaded eyes – a statue of a man that looked like he was pulling on his socks, a graffiti-ed fountain, MacDonald's for pity's sake!

Their problem was that one of them had to take the picture while the other two posed. This was followed by repositioning and differing combinations. There was no way that they could get all three of them in a photo together without the help of an outside agent. Photos are serious business to the Japanese and this was a failing.

This was my chance! Take a photo of them all and just happen to bust out my "impeccable" Japanese. They'll be awestruck by my unexpected yet wholly welcome language skills and then in the ensuing flurry of bows and "yoroshiku onegai shimasu[32]"'s what could be more natural than to offer them my phone number and e-mail address just in case they have any problems. There'd surely be some arcane bits of English life admin they would need help with so they'd contact me and slowly we'd develop a friendship. Catch people while they're vulnerable – that was the way forward. I'd forged acquaintances and made commitments in my first few weeks in Japan that were still haunting me seven years later. Ha! Payback time!

I composed a few sample sentences in my head and started the short walk towards them. I attempted a confident stroll...

I stopped dead in my tracks – I could speak decent enough Japanese but my one handed photo taking skills were sadly lacking. I could probably stand up without my stick but I would have to get somebody to hold it or find somewhere to prop it up. Then keeping a camera steady one handed had been beyond me when I'd been practising alone in my room, those snaps that weren't totally blurred were so badly framed as to be useless.

I can speak Japanese but I can't take a decent fucking photo!

---

[32] よろしくお願いしま – a sort of general "nice to meet you, please act kindly towards me" kind of phrase. Maybe the most used phrase in Japanese?

Crestfallen, I turned tail and shuffled towards my bus stop. The comforting, mellifluous sound of Japanese was soon out of earshot. It had begun to get cold and the sky was darkening. My bus was late.

Chapter 35

8th November 2009 – 2 years and 2 months since the crippling

Barrow upon Soar, Leicestershire, England

"Shinitai!" [33]

It's a relief to say it to someone other than my therapist after all this time thinking it in isolation. I don't want to scare Jun but I feel better for articulating it in sound rather than just thought.

"Jisatsu shinai kedo shinpai shinaide" [34]

I'm pretty anxious that Jun doesn't misinterpret me. In my limited experience it's always a fairly difficult conversation when you choose to discuss this stuff. I've had conversations with therapists and doctors laced with hidden meanings. When you're so desperate to assert your intelligence at every turn, yearning to prove that your stroke didn't affect any of your higher functions, health professionals, desperate not to patronise or offend, tend to credit me with being brighter than I actually am. There have been a few conversations about self harm and surreptitious glances at my wrists. I don't want Jun to worry about me. I don't expect her to *do* anything to make my life better. I like talking

---

[33] 死にたい – "I want to die"

[34] 自殺しないけど心配しないで – "I won't commit suicide though don't worry"

to her but don't want her to feel powerless and guilty. I do that quite enough for the two of us.

Our weekly Skype chats were something I looked forward to. Me gurning into the camera built into the top of my laptop screen. Placing my face in all the comedy filters the webcam software had to offer trying to disguise the fact that I had very little positive to talk about. Jun, crap new computer unable to cope with both audio and video, a disembodied voice crackling over the Wi-Fi. I was a pretty repressed gaijin and Jun was a fairly open minded Japanese so, when we were living together, we met halfway in terms of communicating and talking about ikky things like feelings. Now we were apart and I had little chance to do anything but self-obsess we didn't communicate as well. She seemed to be becoming more stereotypically Japanese and my overflowing emotions demanded expression to somebody I felt I could still really talk to. I had a million things I wanted to say but I tried not to.

I was a little scared that taking too many blocks out of my seawall could lead to a terrifying emotional tsunami that would wash Jun away completely. I told Jun the truth but I was careful to limit how much I shared at any one time. Better a few drips of truth rather than a tidal wave. Jun, on the other hand, either had an awful life back with her parents or was embarrassed to admit that things were inching towards ok for her. She didn't seem much happier than me most weeks.

Reminiscing was a safe conversation topic as well as the health of our Sai who Jun had custody of now. I would try to explain the intricacies of the British benefit system or about that photography course I was doing, all in my faltering, eroding Japanese. Not only were we losing things to talk about we were even losing the tools of communication. Japanese had been our main language but I was beginning to forget it. I'd gone from speaking and hearing Japanese all day everyday to only hearing it once a week. Jun's English was serviceable. We had lost that "understanding what you mean just because I know you so well rather than you are actually explaining it at all comprehensibly in language" thing which had served us so well in the past.

So I would desperately waltz around my life for fear of scaring Jun off, not even calling on particularly bad days, but sometimes it would all just gush out, snot splattering the keyboard, my crying face incongruously superimposed in the centre of a sunflower. This time it was coming out.

"Shinitai I just want to die, Jun, but I'm not going to commit suicide or anything"

My Japanese couldn't cope too well with this level of vocabulary needed but it felt brilliant to tell someone especially as Jun seemed happy enough to accept this at face value. She didn't seem shocked or feel compelled to give me a long list of reasons why my life was really worth living. She didn't say anything really. What could you say that wasn't a cliché or a platitude? Just saying the words out loud felt good but they weren't much use as a conversation starter. As the sounds rushed out of my mouth there was a tangible sense of relief but it was a full stop rather than the start of a fresh conversational paragraph.

This was my dilemma. I didn't want to commit suicide. I couldn't face the pain it would inevitably entail and, besides, I had no idea how to actually do it. I couldn't imagine how you would go about getting a gun. I had plenty of pills that I could take too many of but, as far as I could tell, I would only end up with *really* loose joints or *extraordinarily* thin blood. I couldn't manage the whole noose thing either tying the knot or climbing the stool, not with just the one hand. I don't think I could get in a bath and, anyway, I'd only be able to slit one wrist if I ever got there.

My parents had just gone away for the weekend and that would have been the perfect opportunity to do it but the practicalities eluded me. It was all so messy. I didn't want to ruin my new Ikea sheets. Blood is a bitch to get out. My self-esteem is so shot that I can't imagine that anyone will actually miss me but I can imagine that people I know will feel guilty for not being more supportive, not looking after me more. This would spoil my parents' retirement plans. I make vague ideas to do it after my parents die but that wouldn't be fair on my brother and sisters. Why should they be encumbered with guilt when my parents aren't? Then there's Jun. I know she thinks that she's let me down. In the past she's even said that she thinks the stroke was her fault, that if she had been kinder to me then none of this would have happened. How bad would she feel if I killed myself?

No, I don't want to commit suicide. I just want to cease to exist, to have never been. I just don't want to be here anymore. I wish I could just disappear. I don't want to make anyone else feel bad but I want to feel good for a little while even if that means feeling nothing. I find, the more I think about this, that I tend to feel that consciousness must go on. It can't just flicker out permanently. In that case wherever I went next it couldn't possibly be any worse. A documentary I saw stated that dolphins have to consciously remember to breath or else they die. If humans were like that I would probably have taken that way out a long while ago. I'm a cripple – it's perfectly possible I could just forget to breathe one day. That wouldn't be a huge surprise to anyone. A passive kind of disengagement with life rather than a grand dramatic gesture

The silence at the end of the connection crackles and whirrs but Jun doesn't say anything. I say goodbye and hang up. Next week we talk about benefits and she sends me a photo of the cat.

Chapter 36

6th August 2010 – 2 years and 11 months since the crippling

Barrow-upon-Soar, Leicestershire, England

You're supposed to start the day with the three 's's – shit, shave and shower. Or at least that's how you start the day if you're Larry Blackmon from Cameo being interviewed by "Smash Hits" in 1986 and it had stuck with me since then. I certainly didn't try to put on those airs and act real cool and I did actually have a lot of time for psychological romance but in terms of morning routine I tended to follow Larry's lead. I had been 15 in 1986 so the thought of shaving being an essential part of your morning ablutions was an exciting prospect. It never quite happened, unfortunately. I still can't grow anything more than a sorry-looking goatee and rarely shave more than twice a week. I'm old enough to have a debilitating stroke but not old enough to grow a proper beard – how does that work again? Still I liked to start the day adhering to as many of Larry's instructions as I could. A shower is just good manners and I could normally manage to curl something out even if it tended to take a little while.

I'm perched on the toilet seat staring at the photo frame, lost in thought. This frame was originally on the shelf next to my ever-expanding collection of CD's in Osaka. Now it was on a low window sill in my bathroom in Barrow-upon-Soar next to a fading spider plant. I can't really remember who we got it from but it had been a present. Made of curved glass, it contained slots for four photos – two normal photo size and two of a smaller size. Four photos that happened to be lying round had been shoved haphazardly into the slots and the frame had been bunged on a shelf to receive the odd cursory glance and a very occasional dusting.

The choice of photos had been arbitrary at best but now seemed portentous. Two big ones of me and Jun together and one smaller one of each of us separately. .

The first large picture shows me and Jun somewhere near Kyoto, Arashiyama maybe, in the early autumn. We'd gone to look at the momiji[35]. The crowds were massive and catered for by all kinds of food stalls. This particular spot was in a country park. A lake sat next to the paths and trees with row boats for hire. We'd rented one and headed onto the lake. I was terrible at rowing, falling back in my seat as the oars constantly slipped their slots and rapidly running out of puff. Jun took over and confidently sculled us around the lake. I loved that she was so much more capable than me and I think she did to. Once our time was up we gave the boat back and carried on with our wandering. Someone offered to take our photo against the backdrop of the trees. We look well. Jun still has her long hair and my purple down jacket chimes with the orange leaves. We look happy – I'm grinning a big stupid grin and Jun turns a worry free face to the camera. She looks as though she's about to giggle - probably remembering how bad I was at rowing.

---

[35] 紅葉 – autumn leaves normally on Japanese Maples. Going to scenic spots to view them is traditional and virtually obligatory.

The first smaller picture is Jun alone. She's wearing a dark kimono and is at 90° to the camera. I don't remember what she is doing, where she is going or why she is dressed formally. I didn't take the photo and it always struck me how alien Jun looked, not like the woman I slept with everyday. These kind of clothes I saw so rarely, the lips so red and enticing and her hair, still long, but up in that twin starburst concoction that I loved to unpick so much. She looks ravishing. It always amazed me how this woman I lived and thought I knew so well with could transform herself into a beautiful stranger through a simple act of will.

The other small photo is of me at meal time and taken by Jun from the other side of the table we used to erect when we ate downstairs. Jun is sat at the other end of the table and the top of her plate sneaks into the bottom of the frame. By the looks of it I've cooked sausage and mash. It was part of my limited, rotating menu of things that I could confidently make. Me cooking something palatable was clearly a rare enough occurrence that Jun felt the need to document it for posterity. I'm toasting the camera with a glass of what looks like umeshu[36]. I'm enviously thin, confident in a pink t-shirt and smiling goofily. In the background is an unconnected computer monitor suggesting we've only just moved in and not quite unpacked. That was a great time. I felt like I was taking giant strides to adulthood. I didn't just "have" a girlfriend, I "lived" with her like a real grown-up might.

The final photo is my favourite. Me and Jun on Miyajima near Hiroshima in front of the big red temple gates standing in the sea. It was our first trip away together, still getting to know each other but more and more delighted with what we found. We're stood side by

---

[36]梅酒 - plum liquor: a brief obsession because it was a drink we both liked. Neither of us like wine much so a drink we could share was a welcome novelty.

side. Japanese culture is less tactile than the West so there's no arms around shoulders but Jun pinches my wrist gently. It looks like a gesture of possession and I look happy to be owned. We're trying to look insouciant in sunglasses but I remember being soaked in sweat and keen for some air-conditioned respite. To my joy Jun felt the same. Many Japanese people just coped with the heat as a fact of life but Jun was thrillingly intolerant of it.

I want to dive into those photos and live in that glossy 2-D world for ever. I understand conceptually that life moves on and maybe I should as well but I don't want to. Life was so much better then, so much easier to live. What is wrong with celebrating that, once upon a time, my life was good? That, not so long ago, I was capable of living a life like everyone else. Often 10 minutes contemplating these snaps will make the day a write off – nothing more than endless journeys through the backstreets of pre-stroke memories followed by tears and self-recrimination.

Other times I stare at the pictures and try to think of bad things related to them – the bangers and mash wasn't actually that nice and why wasn't I invited to wherever Jun was going in the kimono? I try to persuade myself that I wasn't really happy back in those days – the sun was always too hot and me and Jun sometimes argued. This is very true. I have a wonderful talent for being miserable in most situations and not knowing what was going to happen in a few years I didn't appreciate what that these were the best days of my life. I thought things would be like this forever. That this was the norm. If you'd stopped me in the street then and asked me if I was happy I'm not sure what I would have said at the time but I now know without the slightest shred of doubt that I was happier than I am *now*.

I talk about the photos with my counsellor. About how I can integrate my past into my present. Neither of us really have a clue but we settle on a simple idea – I start each day with 10 minutes silent meditation on them. All I do is try not to feel bad as I look at them. This is all part of my life and I can try to integrate it into my personal narrative. I probably can't but I can try. Everybody has happier and sadder times in their life but, for me, the contrast and the chasm is just too huge to contemplate or comprehend. Maybe one day?

I finish my shit, wipe my arse and hobble back into my bedroom. I'm often exhausted and totally drained by the time I reach the breakfast table.

Part 7

Chapter 37

16th October 2009 – 2 years and 1 month since the crippling

Shepherd's Bush, London, England

This is still new enough to be an adventure. My mum drops me and the chair off at the station and I roll around looking forlorn until a staff member comes to rescue me. He's gruff and friendly, leading me across the tracks and positioning me at the spot on the platform that tallied up with where the wheelchair spot on the train would end up. He left but said he would be back with the ramp in good time to get me on the train.

The train was only a minute or two late and the guy appeared on cue to roll me up the slope onto the train. Once on board the end of the corridor is difficult to negotiate, narrow and twisty but once among the seats things are better. The spot designated for me is an empty space with a table. Just enough room for my chair and no one else so my peace and privacy are assured. Maybe if I was travelling mob-handed this might seem isolationist and divisive but I'm travelling alone and so I'm perfectly happy. Getting the chair flush with side of the train and not protruding into the walkway is tricky. Parallel parking was never my forte but my chair is light enough that I can do a kind of sideways bunny hop until I'm where I need to be. I slip the brakes on, manage to untangle my headphone cable and clip the plastic "page holder opener" thing over my book. The train pulls out of the station and soon begins to pick up speed. Fields roll by and I feel wonderful, in motion and kinetic. Air France in my ear perfectly suits my mood. I'm rereading "Girlfriend in a Coma". It's about my favourite book and its familiarity is reassuring. The conductor stamps my ticket and offers to fetch me something from the buffet car.

The train rushes through the countryside. It stops sometimes – Leicester, Bedford, Kettering, Luton Parkway. I've passed through all these stations tens of times over the years but their newness to new me tingles my retinas. I go plenty of places but I don't really cover any distance. I rarely go anywhere new: home to various hospitals, home to the City Ground, home to the cinema. Plenty of places but so rarely anywhere different. Part of this is that I'm terrified of anywhere that I don't know. Multiple untold hazards swim in my mind – staircases, kerbs, crowds. I like to know the lie of any land I have to traverse. My risk assessment radar works so much better if I know the terrain involved. This is limiting but it does mean that anything that tempts me out of my shell must be fairly enticing to seem worthwhile. Tonight is. Saint Etienne at Shepherd's Bush Empire. Probably my favourite band playing my favourite album of theirs through in order first song to last. I've loved the twists of their career, the smorgasbord of their influences and that while they were never afraid of dance music they never forgot to include a tune that your milkman could whistle. Plus the fact they had the decency to release some Japan-only albums while I was living there. A Friday night gig and the knowledge that Martin and Helen, who live near St Pancras and who I had been to stay with before since the stroke, would be interested as well sealed the deal.

The train pulled into St Pancras and all the able-bodied passengers got off. I'm supposed to wait until someone appears with a ramp to get me off. This is done after everyone else has left so you're sat there lonely until someone rescues you. Today it takes a long time. The carriage lights go off and I'm sat in sudden darkness. I begin to suspect I've been forgotten about. It's no more than a minor inconvenience though. The worst that could happen is that I wouldn't be found until cleaners arrived to sort the train out. Embarrassing for all concerned but nothing more. We've got plenty of time before the concert. I sit back in my chair and put my earbuds back in. Eventually a sheepish looking employee appears and snaps me out of my reverie. He wheels me onto the platform where Martin and Helen are waiting.

I love Martin and Helen. Friends from university, I was slightly responsible for them hitting it off nearly 20 years ago. They've been together ever since. I'm proud of this tiny contribution I made to the sum total of human happiness on the planet. It's great to see them. We do the awkward hugging moment. How exactly is the best way to hug someone in a wheelchair when one of his arms doesn't work terribly well? I don't get a lot of tactile interaction these days. I love it when I do and worry that my physical incompetence appears as diffidence. I've visited Martin and Helen before so we've already got the basics of what to do for me sorted out. Martin knows not to push the chair unless I ask but he's always ready to be jump in when required. It's actually quite nice to be pushed about by a mate of 20 years standing. Some things change and some things stay the same. They've just moved into a new house that's no more than walking distance from the station so we just roll and walk back. They've acquired a dog since last time I came down so, once I get in the house, the first job is to get acquainted. I'm playing with the dog in the kitchen and catching up with Martin and Helen. I'm stood up in the centre of the room and I feel like I'm taking up too much space so I just take a little step back. Suddenly, inexplicably I'm on my arse on the floor. I've somehow toppled backwards and fallen. I attempt to get up before anything happens but Martin is on me in a flash, arm hooked under a shoulder to hoist me up again. Helen wants to know if I'm hurt. I'm fine, more embarrassed than anything else. I fall occasionally but rarely indoors. I would like to blame something – slippy lino or a smidgen of dog wee or something – but it was just me. I must have slipped or caught my foot or something. But it's alright. There's no harm done. I'm among friends in this cosy kitchen and nobody is judging me. I'm disabled now. Sometimes I fall over. That's just how it is. It doesn't mean anything. No point in over-analysing. We have time for a quick takeaway before we go and Helen tells me about her recent lecturing trip to China.

The taxi arrives in good time, a people carrier with plenty of space for all of us and my wheelchair. It seems ridiculously cheap for a trip clear across London and we give him a decent tip. After some confusion over which particular side door we're supposed to use we get in. No queues for us just a shiny ramp. It's a standing gig but we're positioned at the back of the hall by the bar in a cosy little alcove. No chance of moshing but the view is great. It's not a designated "disabled" area or anything. We keep a few would-be space invaders back with glares and elbows.

The show is great. Glitter and sequins. Memories and nostalgia. Spoken-word samples and lovers-rock bass lines. The show ends and I buy a t-shirt. We troupe out down the shiny slide by the side door. It's a cool evening. Neon lights the street and the road is still busy with cars. The tempting smell of a burger van wafts from somewhere unseen. The taxi arrives and ferries us back to King's Cross. On the sofa in the lounge I'm about done, eyes drooping and neck starting to roll back uncontrollably. I'm tired, a happy exhaustion. This is way more fun than I've had in a long time. I say my goodnights and head upstairs. I need my sleep. The fun's not over – tomorrow me and Marts are up to the City Ground and the football.

Chapter 38

27th April 2010 – 2 years and 8 months since the crippling

Barrow upon Soar, Leicestershire, England.

Things have been good the last few months between me and Jun. I have enough going on that I can usually rustle up a decent conversation. I don't have the language skills to discuss the intricacies of my course (it's really noticeable how bad we are both becoming at each other's native language. I was so proud of my Japanese. It's another shame in a life full of them) but spending time with younger folks in all their exuberance and energy is common ground. Most people on my course are a lot younger and a lot of Jun's colleagues are in their early twenties. Plus she's taken an evening job in a bar so the assorted bar flies and salary men whose glasses she refills give us another thing to talk about.

There's still a lot of awkward small talk. Well, it seems awkward to me after the intimacies we had before but that's what we have to share now. Delicious meals, desire for a holiday and impending colds are the types of thing we talked about and those kind of subjects must make up a proportion of the conversations held most days by most people in the developed world. You can't talk about the big issues all the time every day. There's also a lot of genuine laughter on both sides – the shared indignities bought about through living with your parents in your thirties, my lack of common sense and Jun's inexplicable desire to watch the later films in the Saw series. Jun never initiates conversations about my stroke but she tries to engage with me when I do. I'd like her to talk to me about it a bit more but I'm beginning to understand that it's hard for everyone not just Jun. Where do you start? What do you say? What if you say the wrong thing? Perhaps he doesn't want to talk about it? I do want to talk about it. It quite often feels like the only thing I do have to talk about. As isolated and lonely as I feel most of the time I kind of understand. I'm pretty fucking weird especially if you've known me *before*. Before I became me I'd never met anyone even remotely like me.

I regularly made a point of reminding Jun that she could go and use my passport to go and get the divorce whenever she wanted. I'm sure she didn't need reminding and I'm sure she'd been keeping the photocopy in a safe place since I had sent it a year and a bit earlier but it felt right to occasionally let her know that I was still happy for her to do it. Last summer she had gone to a wedding and sent me some photos of her looking spruced up. She hadn't been wearing her wedding ring in the photos. At this point I was still wearing mine. I liked the fact that my stroke arm held my wedding ring and also the Paul Smith watch she'd got me for that first hospital birthday. Somehow the fact that she'd bought the watch while I was still "normal" and given it to me after the stroke seemed important. I just liked having a bit of my body that was still linked to Jun.

Those wedding photos were great. Jun looked hot in a pistachio dress and matching chiffon scarf around her neck. She looked sexy and grown-up and kind. In one photo she was playing with a baby in a pushchair and her expression was so loving and caring. Transmitting and receiving joy equally. It was a tiny glimpse of a life we could never have. I didn't notice the lack of a ring to begin with. I was getting on with my day doing my therapist-prescribed stretches when the thought suddenly occurred to me and I was sent rushing back to the computer. There were four photos. On two Jun was stood in a group and her left hand was obscured but It was obvious on the photo with the baby when I clicked onto full 2592x1944 pixel resolution. Jun was crouched down to the side of the pushchair and her ringless finger was clear. Leaving the taunting photo on the desktop I took to my bed expecting the tears to follow.

To my surprise I felt kind of......alright. No tears were forthcoming and I got on with my stretching exercises fetching my stick and using it to unwind my shoulder. I spent the rest of the day much like any other. I walked up to the cash machine and played Facebook Scrabble with my friend in Reno. I thought about the ring but my over-riding emotion was of acceptance. I didn't like that the person who had taken my name wasn't wearing the ring that signified it but I couldn't really argue. I hadn't seen Jun for over a year so what right did I have to really be upset if she wasn't identifying herself as my wife anymore? I was angry that she hadn't told me before she sent the photos. I was still wearing my ring and felt a bit pathetic. I had had a bit of a strop and forswore our weekly Skype's for a few weeks but it was more a case of raging against the dying of the light rather than anything specific, a general unfocussed rage. I was upset that Jun hadn't thought to tell me rather than the fact that she'd actually done it.

So when I made one of my routine references to Jun using the passport whenever she wanted and Jun caught me off guard by saying that she'd been having some problems with her tax and she'd probably go and get the divorce done one day next week I was surprised but not particularly upset. I didn't want to get divorced and I wanted Jun to be "Padmore" for ever as an everlasting tribute to our union and as undeniable evidence that once I pulled a cutie and even got her to marry me but there seemed little point trying to put off an inevitable necessity. I didn't know if the tax problems that Jun was talking about were genuine or if she just felt that it was time. If she had tried to explain the intricacies of the Japanese taxation system I wouldn't have understood and I actually wasn't that curious anyway. If that was what we were going to hang things on then that was fine by me.

I didn't like being "divorced". There wasn't a box on forms entitled "divorced through medical necessity". I was pretty sure that this was it for me and relationships. I didn't say anything to anyone aside from my counsellor. I'd stopped wearing my ring after I saw Jun wasn't wearing hers anymore. I'd contemplated wearing it on a different finger as a reminder of how things had been. I was proud of the time I had spent with Jun and I was proud that I had once been a husband but that was a bit too much like living in the past even for me so the ring sat in a drawer to be often fingered and mused upon. No one in my family had mentioned that I wasn't wearing my ring and I had offered no explanation. Similarly I didn't mention this formality. I knew that when my family sent Christmas cards I would have to explain that Jun had gone back to being "Adachi" rather than "Padmore" but I would deal with that when I had to.

I could picture the scene now – telling my mum that I was divorced in as casual a way as possible but however I said it would still elicit the same reply –

"So how do you feel about that? Are you happy about that? Are you OK about it?"

Said with genuine concern, these are reasonable questions but still I have a problem with how to answer them. "How do I feel about that?" - I feel sad but resigned. "Are you happy about that?" – NO! Of course not but what am I supposed to do? I'm powerless about a lot of things nowadays, disenfranchised from my own life. "Are you OK about it?" – that's a weird question to me now, frighteningly irrelevant. The question implies that I have some kind of choice about how I construct my world. I can decide whether to make things "OK" or "not OK". Everything since September 6th 2007 is "not OK". Nothing will ever be "OK" again. There's nothing I can do about this. All I can do is try to accept this and try to live this strange half-life as best I can now. "OK" or "Not OK" is not a choice I have anymore. That is gone. My life doesn't operate in binary oppositions anymore. It's not "good" or "bad" rather a sliding scale of "quite how bad today?"

I don't understand Jun anymore. I don't understand her behaviours or motivations. Don't understand why she would think it was OK to be audibly typing out a report for work while we're trying to Skype. We have good chats: Laughing and sharing reminiscences of favourite meals and holidays. Some days we have bad chats: never getting beyond generic small talk and rote inquiries into the health of family members. But we always try again the week after. I used to think that maybe I did understand her. At least as close as I had come to understanding anybody. Perhaps I did, perhaps I didn't. Now I have no real idea what is going on in her head or her life. She has no obligation to attempt to explain herself to me. That's the challenge facing me and Jun now – loving someone you don't really know anymore.

Chapter 39

23rd August 2010 – nearly 3 years since the crippling

Mountsorrel, Leicestershire, England

The water is always an intriguing sensation, a different covering for my skin, a new kind of encasement. I haven't taken a bath since my stroke. I wouldn't trust myself to get in and out safely anymore so this weekly feeling is pleasantly unusual. My body feels heavier than normal. Even my fully functioning limbs move slower than usual. The extra resistance of the water stops me trying to rush my body along. I'm even more ungainly here but so is everyone else. Walking journeys that need to be made away from the safety of the side are a stumbling combination shuffle and splash. I'm not worried about falling over and drowning though. Paul, my social worker, helps me out with a lot of stuff I need help with from charity funding applications and organising voluntary work to nights out and the lending of Vince Guaraldi CDs but today he's helping me access the swimming pool and he'd be there to drag me up out of the water if I fell over. Funny how it's so much easier to accept help from people that aren't your parents.

So he's by my side, not close enough to imply that I can't do it myself but near enough to catch me if I fall. Not asking me if I need help when I don't, belittling me with kindness and expectation, but ready to jump in if required. Not giving me a touch-less embrace as if willing me to make use of those outstretched arms. When you need so much help everyday you become very sensitive to exactly how it is given. It probably says more about my own state of mind than anything else but I've become expert in interpreting "help", the semantic range of succour, the semiotics of support. Paul is good at helping without you feeling patronised and powerless.

The pool is busy today. Kids screaming their joy as they dare each other to new achievements. Toddlers giggling uncontrollably as Mum lifts them in and out of the water. I say hello and smile to a few of the regulars I see every week. Today is school holiday-busy but usually it's just me and a few retirees that come at the same time every week. We've started to recognise each other, comrades in our exertions. We'll exchange friendly hellos, bonded by a common endeavour. Once we're in the pool I'm busy doing my lengths but Paul gets chance to chat a bit more while he's waiting for me. The oldsters are cool - camaraderie under tattoos and paunches, gentle encouragement in goggles. One guy notices that I'm getting faster week by week. I actually believe him. I can swim faster than some of them too. To be better than anybody able-bodied at anything at anything physical is pretty astonishing to me.

I raise my arms, one perfect and one acceptable. I can lift my left arm above my head well enough but my elbow tends to flop to 90° if unattended. Still today this doesn't matter. Paul straps the float around my chest. For now I use something to keep me safe and buoyant but when he kids go back to school and the pool gets quieter I'll try a few lengths without the float. It'll be hard work but I think I'll be able to do it. To my initial surprise float technology had progressed in the twenty years since I last used one. Gone are the suspiciously-discoloured white polystyrene oblongs of my youth. The one I use is long, thin and goes across my back. It's held in place by an adjustable strap across my chest. I pull the cord tight and squirm under the rope into the designated "Lane Swimming" area. One deep breath and I'm off.

Over a couple of sessions of high-level experimentation me and Paul worked out my best swimming technique. Float strapped on, I do a personalised remix of a backstroke. My right arm and leg are fine, obviously, and my left leg kicks after a fashion but my left arm still won't make a 360° revolution so I can't do anything with it. It rests on my hip or above my head, enjoying the ride. I first thought that this lob-sided method would mean that I would just go round and round in circles and never move forward but it seems to work. I don't go fast but I cover the water well enough. The distances I cover have slowly built up – 6 lengths, 10, 15, 20, 500 metres then 750. My next target will be a full kilometre. I wish I'd totted up how far I had swum since I began. I must have swum the Channel by now. The Paralympics are safe for a little while but I am getting noticeably smoother. Backstroke means I can't really see other swimmers but Paul generally swims interference for me. Navigation is pretty easy – keep the side of the pool on your left one way and then the lane dividing rope does the same thing on the way back. I do no less than 20 lengths, more if I'm in the mood. I don't want to flog myself but I like to get the exhilaration of proper tiredness.

Horizontal in the water, as long and flat as I can get, I stare up at the corrugated iron on the roof. Some days it's a slog and I have no excess energy for anything aside from spluttering and keeping going but on other days I *transcend*. It's a magnificent feeling and the distance flies by. I experience a serenity and clarity of thought that's denied to me at other times. My mind flutters peacefully around the different parts of my body. Rare feelings of calm and tranquillity course through me. My body is supported, different from other days. Gravity and mass take on new forms. I don't feel as fat as I usually do. I have ideas. I'm alone but that's how I prefer to be right now. I want to get my head back, do my lengths and revel in the exaltation.

Finished, I stop at the shallow end. Paul joins me. He times me. I'm a tiny but significant bit quicker this week. Slowly and clumsily I edge towards the steps. It's harder work this time. I'm tired and wobbly. The change in resistance, water to air, confuses my body every time. Paul passes me my stick and I totter over to the wide window sill and sit down. I need a few minutes to recover before I attempt the longer walk back to the changing room. We sit on the ledge, sun warming our backs, and chat about different things – Paul's 7" jukebox, my old life in Japan, my course, how some of his other clients are getting on. Obviously it's a client/server kind of relationship but I feel like Paul genuinely likes me. I enjoy our chats and I think he does too. In spite of everything it's like talking as equals. A lady walks past and says hello. She's seen us here deep in conversation for a few weeks and grins – "Women are supposed to be the gossips!" she laughs.

Reverie broken we head back to the changing rooms and get changed. My damp trunks and towel go in the massive white Adidas bag which has somehow followed me back from Japan, a loyal and faithful companion. It's far too big really but its role is more than just carrying kit. It links me back to my old life. Futsal may not be possible anymore but I can swim instead. It's not as much fun but it'll do. I'm tired but justified. Paul drops me off at home. I treat myself to some already calorie-offset cookies and have a snooze before tea. My feeling of inner warmth and weary contentment lasts all evening. I still don't have much to do but after my exertions there's nothing I particularly feel like doing. I'm comfortably weary rather than the itchy, irritable tiredness I experience most nights. Normally I watch football because I have nothing better to do. It fills dead evenings and weekend time. I enjoy it but before it was always a binary opposition. There was often something else going on at the same time so that meant finding the time to watch the match was a treat. Now most of the time I'd like to have something to do so I *can't* watch it but tonight all I want to do is to curl up on the sofa with Monday Night Football. So that's precisely what I do.

Chapter 40

20th September 2010 – 3 years since the crippling

Barrow upon Soar, Leicestershire, England

Bedtime. Sometimes Sesame the cat comes to join me. Even after over two years here I'm still getting to know him. Ses is getting old now but I have been away for most of his life. I still don't quite feel at home here. This wasn't a place of my choosing. I don't really know the names of the streets around the village. Apart from a few exploratory rambles I only really go from home to bus stop or post-box and then back again. Bumping into an acquaintance of Paul's at the pool we find that we both live in Barrow. We swap the names of the streets where we live. She knows exactly where I am. I have no idea where she stays.

Nevermind. This is what I do know: this house and its inhabitants from the baby swallows in the nest under the eves to the random neighbourhood cat that sometimes spends the night in our kitchen. There are advantages in being the guy who doesn't go out too much. All the animals recognise me as a constant in their lives and treat me with much affection. I can always be guaranteed to have a spare minute to give them a cuddle or a snack. Ses likes me and I like him. He's ginger like Sai but with a white underbelly. He's more of a peachy ginger whereas Sai is more pumpkin or persimmon. Ses strikes me as weird in that he's happy to be stroked but won't ever sit on your lap. Sai will jump on your lap the moment you sit down and that always struck me as a fundamental obligation on the cat side of the human/feline contract. But then our Japanese house had no central heating so my lap was probably the warmest place in the house back then. Now Ses can stay warm anywhere without being stroked by me every last second. Tactile contact is great up to the moment it starts to grate. Ses is curled like an ammonite on my duvet when I slide under. He's down by my left foot and I'm trying not to wake him. Turns out he wasn't asleep after all. He uncurls himself, arches his back and moves further up the bed to within stroking range. I read my Kindle for a little, marvelling with every virtual page turn about how much better it is now I don't have to wrestle a book into dog-eared, broken-spined submission every time I fancy a few chapters before bed.

When it comes time for lights off I put the Kindle away, set Kraftwerk going almost inaudibly and switch off my bedside lamp. Ses stands up again to accommodate my little wriggles but doesn't make any move to get off the bed. He's been here a hundred times before and he knows the routine. Light off, I snuggle down the bed and Ses tucks himself in by my left arm. In all my time back here Ses has not yet understood that my left arm and hand don't work quite like everyone else's. Every time he comes to me for some love he tries to bury his head under my left hand and nuzzles as though he's trying to coax the limb back into life. I can stroke him, after a fashion, with my left arm but my touch is so heavy handed and my hand-to-fur aim is so scattershot that I eventually stop trying and just reach over with my right. However much space I leave on my right hand side he'll never sit over there. He likes the left side of me and nothing will convince him otherwise.

I stroke Ses for a little while. He barely moves under my fingers but the gentle purring noise signals his appreciation. The reassuring head heaviness comes just as the distant murmuring of the "Autobahn" reaches its final junction.

An unignorable call from within my boxer shorts wakes me up a while later. Reaching for my mobile I see the time "1.37am". I yawn and get unsteadily to my feet. Ses is waiting patiently by the door and I let him out. He doesn't like to spend the whole night confined in my room. I don't like to sleep with the door ajar so he can't get out on his own but I'll normally wake up sometime in the night for just long enough to let him out. The system seems to work well enough. I get to feel secure while I sleep and he doesn't seem too bothered about waiting. He comes into my room at bedtime plenty.

I stagger to the toilet and crash land on the seat. Bleary-eyed dead of night walking is much harder than the usual. Shoes tossed casually on to the floor becoming potentially life- threatening obstacles. Walls, cupboards and door frames become handy balance keepers. Any shame bought about my trips and stumbles though are quickly erased by the return to sleep. I got to the toilet or bedroom door safely – that's the important thing. On the seat I look at the four photos of me and Jun rubbing along lopsidedly in a single frame – one standing in front of the huge red torii in the sea at Miyajima and another of us blending into the autumn foliage at Arashiyama. I smile to myself. Those were grand times. Clearly much better than now but those days are gone forever. I'll always keep those memories in a lacquer-ware box deep in the safest corner of my mind but that's all they are now –

memories of better days. The fact that my life before the stroke was rich and a homely kind of spectacular mean that now it's inevitable that I feel an unbridgeable chasm between here and there. As difficult is that is to take, it shows that I was living my life along the right lines. Having this awful trauma occur and then not missing the life you led before would show that old life up as a desiccated husk.

And in the silence of the early hours the constantly critical, whining voice that rises up from somewhere deep has been not been woken by my toilet trip. Somewhere it lies and snores shallowly. The relative silence allows another voice to be heard, quiet but insistent. This is what it says –

"You're doing alright. What happened was unexpected and unfair. It shouldn't have happened to you. It shouldn't happen to anyone but it does and this time it happened to choose you. That's not a judgement. You haven't done anything to deserve this. It's not your fault. You're not being punished for something. You're just very, very unlucky. It just happened. It has no meaning at all. It just *is*.

And this isn't a race to be won. You're not competing with anyone. If you're happy with how you are doing then that's enough. That's all there is now. The way people judge a life doesn't apply to you anymore. I know it sounds stupid but, in a way, you're free. No one knows how this feels except you. No one. You haven't given up. You keep trying to do positive things however small they seem. It's hard. Sometimes things you try will work. Sometimes they won't but you'll keep trying. That's just how things are going to be now. Victories and defeats. Successes and failures."

A small but undeniable calm settles over me like a light dusting of snow and I head back to bed looking forward to the undisturbed hours before my alarm interrupts me. I pass my chest of drawers on the way back. On one side of the speaker are the massed ranks of my pills but on the other are my incense sticks and a bowl to burn them in.

Incense was always a small but constant part of my life in Nakatsu. Every payday I would head over to the Loft department store and stock up on my monthly essentials – a supply of stickers for the kids in my lessons and my stash of Autumn Twilight. They are made by a centuries old company from Kyoto and I settled on that brand because it seemed to have a sense of Japanese refinement rather than any New Age hippy vibe. I initially got the pack that was a mixture of scents meant to represent each season but I quickly settled on the autumnal. It was a rich, heavy smell just the right side of pungent. I only ever lit one last thing at night and it was my way of signalling to no one in particular that my day was done. As the tiny plume of smoke unfurled about us it seemed to create a somnolent atmosphere that matched and enhanced my mood. It was always my thing. Jun didn't mind the smell too much but it wasn't her favourite. She knew it was one of those important little things that made up my character, inconsequential from the outside but almost essential from the inside, and always made sure we burnt it when I was allowed home for weekends during my hospital time. Once, when I was in the hospital, she sent me a mobile phone picture of a stick burning in its holder. It reassured me that away from this lonely place and its strange bed my real life was still out there somewhere.

Here in England it was impossible to get hold of. Sometimes Jun sent me a couple of packets but it was never enough to last long. I didn't ration it, greedy to recreate a tiny part of my old life. Gradually my care packages dried up. I think maybe the company stopped selling into other shops and just sold out of their own store. Anyway it stopped appearing and although I was certain that nothing else could compare I still liked a tiny bit of ritual last thing at night. Reluctantly I headed to the web. Most online incense stores are a horrible combination of headshop and snake oil salesman but I eventually found some new kinds to try. All Japanese, of course. For some reason one of my classy Japanese packs of sticks was out of stock and they arbitrarily replaced it with an Indian brand complete with vulgar, prancing statues on the packaging. Over the next few weeks I carefully sampled these new fragrances and attempted to remember my opinions in the morning – Kodo Morning Star Pine – nice but a little too wimpy, Herb & Earth Bamboo Incense Cedar – too much dusty remnant for too little noticeable fragrance, Sandalwood Supreme Indian Masala Incense – surprisingly rich and it hung satisfyingly in the air. I had been surprised that I liked the Indian one best of all. I had expected it to smell of halls of residence and woolly conversation but it seemed to suit me best.

I paused and lit one. I had burnt one earlier so two in one night is a little extravagant but I'm trying to be a bit gentler with myself these days. This stick probably cost 20p so I can afford it. Back in bed I switch the light off. The tip of the stick glows comfortingly in the darkness and soon the fragrance reaches my nostrils. I like it. It curls out gentle wisps of husky cinnamon, freshening up the slightly musty locked-in night air. Cleansing but with a tiny mulled spiciness. It reminds me of bonfires and slices of lemon floating on top of bowls of thick purpley wine. It's different from the Autumn Twilight I used to love but it's OK. Not better. Never better but acceptable. Sometimes that has to do.

Sometimes that's enough. Sometimes that has to be enough. Sometimes that's all we have.

2859995R00143

Printed in Great Britain
by Amazon.co.uk, Ltd.,
Marston Gate.

Halfway Gone

Englishman Matt is 35 and happy, loving his life in Japan and his new wife. Then, one Thursday morning before work, his life changes forever. Part memoir and part travelogue, "Halfway Gone" is a story of life and love before and after a stroke. As funny as it is sad, as heart-warming as it is heart-breaking and it's all true!

ISBN 9781470945893
90000 >
9 781470 945893